A Chip on My Shoulder

EUGENE ROSS

PAGE PUBLISHING
Conneaut Lake, PA

First originally published by Page Publishing 2024

ISBN 979-8-89157-877-7 (pbk)
ISBN 979-8-89157-878-4 (digital)

Printed in the United States of America

To my wife, Marjorie, who shared this story in many ways.

A B O U T   T H I S   S T O R Y

This is, on the surface, a story about my early life and experiences that I had as a young man and pilot. However, it is my intention to tell the story of men who were dedicated to this country, ready to give their lives if necessary, but were, as to many that I encountered, left with little or no future in the Air Force even though they had served in critical time in our history when we needed to present a competent, prepared deterrent to a fearsome challenge, the Soviet Union.

Our flying jobs, tanker crews, do not bring to mind the glamourous scarf-wearing or fifty-mission cap-wearing bomber pilot headed for certain promotion.

But they made it all work.

My part was indeed small, but as I look back on my life, in which I have done many things, this is what I am proud of. This was for my country, a great thought to take to the grave when the time comes. I feel I must include the events in my life that eventually, for better or worse, shaped my early years in such a way as to make flying a welcome and productive thing for me.

As I tell my story, I include my perceptions of what was happening around me not only in and around my Air Force environment, but what was happening on the world stage as I perceived it.

I have changed the name of my squadron friends to avoid intrusion into their lives, except for two, Major John Purdy, who became my flying companion and best friend, and James Mclaughlin, my primary flying instructor and someone who taught me not only real flying but how to be a pilot. There is a difference. Notwithstanding what I have put into words below, all my squadron members were dedicated men who did the best they could.

But to begin…

It was October of 1962 and more or less a typical fall day at Ellsworth Air Force Base just outside Rapid City, South Dakota. My wife, Marge, twenty-five at that time, as well as my two children, Mark and Marissa, lived in a two-bedroom home on a gently winding street lined with residences on both sides and could easily have been taken for a typical suburban setting in towns and cities in America. The big difference was that this was all located on an Air Force base and provided housing on base for officers and their families assigned to the base to provide aircrews for the B-52 bombers and KC-135 air-refueling tankers, then a critical part of the US nuclear deterrence program, which fell heavily on the US Strategic Air Command with the national goal of controlling the Soviet threat.

On that particular fall day at the base, one thing was noticeable about that neighborhood setting.

The residents had, for the most part, disappeared.

A major international crises was occurring. The Soviet government, with Nikita Khrushchev in the lead, was arming Cuba with nuclear-capable missiles, making a large portion of the US, including our base, subject to nuclear attack.

It was called the Cuban Missile Crisis.

Ellsworth was considered a major target in the event of war, and the base resident dependents were advised to evacuate.

They did, leaving the street deserted since the husbands were on twenty-four-hour duty on the flight line and not easily able to communicate.

Only one adult and two children remained—my, wife, Marge, and our son and daughter.

C H A P T E R 1

Uncle Ray and the Zephyr

In 1959, while I was part of a KC-97 tanker squadron in Little Rock AFB, and having then established myself as a pilot who fit in well to the life of flying and potential career officer, I came across a fellow copilot from Chicago, who was only a short time from getting out of the service and could not wait. He stopped me in the hall at the squadron building. "What is a college-educated person like you doing making a career doing this? Certainly you could do better in business on the outside."

Good question. The answer is complicated. It is one that took me seven years to find.

In looking back, this whole flying thing started as an escape from my father and stepmother as a young boy. Later in life, with my wife, Marge, I opened a successful business, participated successfully in local politics (both of us were elected to office), traveled the world, having visited all seven continents, participated in national championships, and raised two wonderful and gifted children. Yet at this time of my life, my most significant and cherished memories (excluding Marge and my dogs) was the years I spent strapped into an airplane seat. They were not about my home life.

I was born in Oakland, California, along with my twin brother in late 1934. My mother, a beautiful and gifted woman who had

1

recently obtained a master's degree in psychology from the University of California, died in childbirth. My brother Sylvan was born first and I second. My father, as I learned when I accidentally overheard a telephone conversation, blamed me for her death since I was last born.

My father was, in many ways, a mystery to me. He was distant and demanding of my brother and I and then of me after my brother's death in a hiking accident when we were twelve. He was born to a Polish immigrant couple who farmed him out to a Mormon family in Idaho since they could not afford to raise him, as they also did with his brother and sister. He really had no example of how to raise children. My brother and I were boarded early in our lives, first with my mother's family, who lived in Martinez, California, a small town located just northeast of San Francisco in the Bay Area, on the bay shoreline, and the place to where I returned with my family after I left the service, and then due to the exigencies of WWII, with strangers whom he paid in the Wilmington, California, area (the Port of Los Angeles), where we went to elementary and junior high school. There he managed a hotel and owned the restaurant attached to it. Later, after having a success in the hospitality business, he purchased a nice home and moved us in after returning from having served in the army. He immediately married.

His new wife, who was very pretty, was not a happy stepmother, and our lives became complicated. When my brother died in an accident at age 12, our lives seemed to go downhill after that. My dad lost interest in his business, began gambling, and soon we had to sell the house and move into a rental. I felt like an outcast seeking shelter.

His gambling habit haunted him for the rest of his life, and he eventually died of a heart attack while playing blackjack in a Las Vegas casino.

As soon as we moved in to what was a much smaller home, my stepmother's younger brother came to live with us and had to share my room. Ray, who was a young mechanic (and I think, a good one), had a flair for doing something different. Although apparently living on a low income, he drove a classy Lincoln, which he cared for with a passion. He was also a hobbyist aircraft builder. He and I got along great since he did not much like his sister (my stepmother) either. On Saturdays and Sundays, he would travel to the Compton Airport (in the southern Los Angeles area, as was Wilmington), where he had hangar in which he was rebuilding a Taubman Zephyr, a 1940 vintage midwing, also called a Babcock LC13, with a side by side open cockpit, fabric wings, and side-by-side seating on a wooden plank.

One Saturday, Uncle Ray asked me if I wanted to come along for the day. I was fourteen then, and that day had what was to be a huge impact on my life. I loved working with him and being around the airplanes, trying to be as helpful as I could patching the wings and pumping the throttle when he had to hand crank the propeller to start the plane. When he was ready to fly the plane, he tossed me a helmet with goggles and asked me if I wanted to come along. Of course, I was delighted with the thought, and soon we were flying around the area. I was thrilled. He let me handle the stick and told me how to make turns, which he gently supervised. The plane had a physically connected control stick for each person, so I had my own control device, so it was a good learning setup. I wish I had remembered to find Ray later to tell him what he had instilled in me, but never thought of it until it was too late.

My relationship with my uncle Ray provided a great escape from a cold and not-too-comfortable household and although unbeknown at that time, was the start of something that would seriously affect my life. At age 14, he gave me a needed positive effect and a something to look forward to.

As I mentioned, things were not going good with my dad, who had gone into hotel management, and we moved a couple of times, once to Reno for a short stay and then Cottonwood, Arizona, to live with my stepmother's family. Finally he managed to lease a motel in Blythe, California, out in the desert along the Colorado River, and off we went to Blythe, where, at age 15, I would stay until I graduated high school. There I would continue to find an escape.

CHAPTER 2

Blythe

lythe, located in what is called the Colorado River Desert and next to the Colorado River in the Palo Verde Valley, was primarily an agricultural area, the "valley" running approximately ten miles wide at its widest portion and maybe over twenty miles long next to the river. The river supplied ample irrigation water, and with sunshine every day, crops grew fast. One approached the town by dropping into the flat valley floor from the rolling and uneven desert to the west. It was also close to the middle of a trip from LA to Phoenix, which, in 1949, could easily take two days. So it was thought to be a good place to run a motel, providing a resting place for travelers.

My father leased a motel called the Monterey Motel and enlisted me to help man the desk and do other chores around the motel. The Monterey Motel was at the east end of the downtown area on Hobsonway, the main street and highway that went through town. Now the freeway bypasses the center of town, so one misses the stores, a pool hall (where I spent a lot of time), and the Majestic Bar (where I tried to spend a lot of time).

The motel had twenty-three units arranged in a semicircle around a lawn that required huge amounts of water to keep green. At the entryway was the typical office, only with a built-in family-type apartment on the second floor, which became my home while I was in Blythe. I was assigned certain hours to serve as a clerk for the operation and thereby relieve my father, especially during the evening hours, but working the motel was a constant thing while on the premises, and my father had plenty of things for me to do.

One of the standing orders from my father was that any non-white patron that pulled in (most business was done in the late afternoon and evening when motorists were thinking about stopping for the day) during my shift in the evening were to be assigned cabin 23, the last cabin on the semicircle and farthest from the office. If that cabin was taken and another nonwhite client showed up, my instructions were to tell them we had no vacancies.

This was a strict order, and to violate it meant some type of punishment. I always have wondered where my father picked this up, but it must have been from his experiences in hotel management in the LA area.

Besides its location between two large cities, I must say that Blythe, at that time, did not seem to have much going for it. Very isolated, about a hundred miles in all directions from a town of any consequence, with minimum services. In 1948, it was not a great place to live. The winters were nice, but summertime was a veritable cloud of bugs and crickets and hot! The high school was located in an old Army Air Corps WWII training facility about five miles north of town.

Two things it did have, however, was a small but first-class movie theater (built for the town by a wealthy rancher) that was cooled by what we called then refrigerated cooling, as opposed to the swamp coolers used everywhere else in town. So in the summer, everyone went to the movies as much as they could. The town also had one other really interesting facility, an active airport just west of town up on the desert plateau that had also been one of the two training facilities for WWII pilots in the Blythe area and a great place for me to get away from the motel and my dad. The other training facility became the high school.

In order to get some money for myself, I got a job in the theater, where I did all sorts of tasks, from changing the letters on the marquee to supervising uniformed usherettes (the best part of the job), running the Tuesday night bingo game, which played to a packed house between the double feature. I soon was promoted to assistant manager and became the boss of six good-looking usherettes. I saved my money, bought a 1932 Ford sedan for transportation, and after a year or so, I headed for the airport in my spare time. There really was not much there except one large hangar that housed a private flying business. The operator of the business, a man I called Mr. Dennis, was happy to give flying lessons to a young man at a cheap rate since there was not a big demand for flying lessons in Blythe.

There I was introduced to the Ercoupe, a small plane seating two side by side like the Zephyr. It had a top speed of about 100 mph. It was a good plane to start a teenager in, but this one had a communications radio that barely functioned. It had a "coffee grinder" crank for tuning to a VHF frequency, and it was very finicky. VHF means "very high frequency," and that was the frequency range used for air-to-ground traffic control.

I also had an unofficial instructor whom I remember as having the name of Jim. Jim was a crop duster who kept his planes at the same facility and made a living dusting the lettuce and melon fields of the valley that stretched out along the valley floor next to the Colorado River. Jim used to take me along on his practice runs in his Piper J3, which I understand is common in that business when preparing for a job. When he was ready for the job, he would then fly his duster in to do the work. Flying under power lines was not a big deal to me then, but I learned better.

I remember flying under power lines next to the fields and sometimes, for fun, using the slower, flexible plane, to herd wild burros in the nearby Mojave Desert.

According to my logbook (which my wife, Marge, found in my paperwork and saved for roughly sixty years), I started my official flying in April of 1951, and the last entry was on May 1952, about a year later. There were no more entries after that because I ran away to college in June of that year, and flying was no longer in my life (at least for four years).

But I am jumping ahead.

While working at the theater, I became friendly with one of the usherettes named Mrytle. Mrytle was cute, had a nice figure, and was the sole drum majorette for the high school band, which got a lot of support from the community because they played at football games, a major source of community pride.

Needless to say, I finished my high school in Blythe, and it was through an unforeseeable chain of events that I then found myself accepted to the University of California, where my mother and two aunts had attended.

Blythe High School, or Palo Verde Valley High, had, as I remember, about 400 students, more than half of which were children of farmers and cowboys and had little interest in school (or had time for it) and did not always show up. Besides, the school was a couple of miles out of town, and if you missed the bus, that was it. Either you had a car or you needed to find a ride to school.

The school had a student council and student officers. It was an offbeat governing system where the students controlled the student union (a 20' by 20' room that allowed students to go there to eat whatever lunch they brought with them and buy a soft drink). The soft drink concession consisted of an old red Coca-Cola tub with an open top. A student named Joe was in charge of the operation. However, if one looked into the tub and below the Cokes, you could see rows of beer cans (or bottles, I don't remember which) that were also for sale.

Since it was the policy of the school that the students ran the student union and the faculty stayed out of the student union, the sale of beer went on for some time.

I would guess that maybe there was 150 students that were serious about their education and showed up. I remember two of these very well. One was a young man that lived by our motel and became my best friend in Blythe (Frank) and Mrytle. Although as I said, there was only a small group of serious students, the football team was another story. Everyone showed up for practice during football season, and the whole town came out for the games. There was a junior college also located on the campus, and a dorm had been created out of one of the old barracks to house the college football team, which included 49 of the 51 students in the college when I was there. The fiftieth was the team manager, and the fifty-first, the cheerleader. Palo Verde JC, as it was called was one of the best JC teams in the state when I was there and a really big deal with the townsfolk, and their games were a big deal. In talking to the players, I found that most of them came from the Midwest. I was told that the football players were sent there to get the grades necessary to transfer to one of the Arizona universities. Meanwhile, they could play for Palo Verde JC. So they won a lot.

I was probably the best and most serious male student in the school, but not popular with the farm group. My good friend Frank was. We made a deal in that he would run for student body president, and I would run for vice president. Since he had decided to run away and join the Air Force, I would be president, and that would help my chances into getting into a college. (Even then there was scheming to get into college!) I was not so interested in college, rather a possible way out of Blythe and my situation.

And that is the way it happened. I became student body president just before the chairman of the school trustees drove into the school parking lot and was confronted with a bunch of empty beer containers. Of course, there was a major reversal of the student union operating policy and the "Coca-Cola" tub was removed from the room. It was suggested that I was cleaning up things, and I was of course, challenged to a fight in the parking lot after school. One of us did not show up, and for the life of me, I cannot remember if it was Joe or me. Since Joe left school that day and never came back, it did not really matter.

In my senior year, one of my teachers helped me apply to UC. I did not make a big deal with my father about that since he would rather I stayed and helped him.

Meanwhile, I was determined to get somewhere with Myrtle, who really was not too impressed with me (I weighed about one hundred pounds, and my ears stuck out). But I got a good idea. As I said, the school was on an old Army Air Corps base, and there was an old concrete tarmac out back used for landing practice during the training days in WWII, and it backed up the girls' gym. I asked Mrytle to go behind the gym during lunchtime, saying I had a surprise for her. So I left school before lunchtime and drove out to the airport, took the Ercoupe I was flying, and flew over to the high school. Taxiing up to the girls' gym, I picked up Myrtle and took her for a short plane ride. That impressed her, and I was convinced that my investment in flying lessons was a good investment. I had impressed her. I was actually surprised that she agreed to go, but I was her boss at the theater, and if you lived in Blythe, you were inclined to try anything that was different.

In the spring of 1952, I was ready to do my solo Cross Country which was required to get a private pilot ticket, which I was still aiming for. The chosen route was a "round robin" from Blythe to Yuma to San Diego (landing at San Diego, Lindbergh Field). Then to Long Beach (landing there) and then back to Blythe. The idea was to do this in the daylight so an early start was required. I did my flight planning using a AAA California road map. With the Colorado River as my guide, I would fly to Yuma, then Highway 8 to San Diego, landing at Lindbergh Field. From there up the coastline to Long Beach Airport (landing there) and then east to Riverside, picking up what is now US 10 and following that out to Blythe. A good "pilotage" navigation. That is what this type of very simple navigation was, following the highways. It was necessary to contact control towers at San Diego and Long Beach, land, and get my logbook signed off.

I was off flying the route with no trouble until I needed to contact the tower at Lindbergh Field in San Diego. I could not get the tower frequency set in the radio, so I landed radio silent just as I always did in Blythe. Coming in over the hill while landing to the west, I was not used to seeing such a big runway, so I ignored it and managed to land on an adjacent taxi strip. That caused some commotion in the tower, and I was visited after I parked by a committee of CAA (now called FAA), people who were concerned I knew what I was doing. That surprised me because I thought I was doing just fine. Nevertheless, one of the group signed my logbook and cleared me to go on to Long Beach. However, they called Long Beach and told them I was coming and also cleared the pattern of aircraft when I took off.

Long Beach was not so bad since I had experience in flying around that area with Uncle Ray, and Compton was right next door. Still they cleared the area, met me at the airplane after I landed, and questioned me about how I was going to get back to Blythe and calling Blythe and talking it over with Mr. Dennis. It was finally decided to let me go. They cleared the pattern again and set me free to go home. I am thinking, looking back, that they probably did not see many seventeen-year-old pilots flying around Southern California alone in those days, although later there were many young pilots around.

I took off, heading toward Riverside, where I would pick up the highway out to Blythe. Visibility was not that good due to haze, and I began to worry that I could find the needed highway but kept flying east at about three thousand feet and did pick up the highway out through Banning and Indio. After that, it was a piece of cake since the visibility cleared up and there was the highway going to Blythe. I was back on my stomping grounds and home for dinner.

CHAPTER 3

Hello, UC Berkeley and Marjorie

During the time I was in Blythe, I had been contacted several times by my mother's family and an aunt Roz (my dad's sister), who all through my childhood kept an eye on me since she didn't feel my father was paying attention to my needs. She was right. I owe her plenty. They urged me go to college in Berkeley, where I would get help from my grandfather there. When I found out I was admitted to Cal, I made arrangements with her to stay at her place in Los Angeles until I went north to school. I told my father that June that I was going to LA to visit my aunt, but did not tell him I was not coming back. I never knew his true feeling about me leaving, but when I called him from LA to tell him I was going north to school, it severed for a while, a troubled relationship.

After Blythe, Berkeley was at the same time awesome and scary. I joined a fraternity (recommended by my family) and knew I had to make good grades to keep getting their help. So I did.

It was required that all male students (not otherwise exempt) join an ROTC of some type, Army, Navy, or Air Force. I did not want Army, and Navy ROTC was by invitation only, it seemed, so Air Force was what was left. I really had not thought about becoming an Air Force pilot then, but I had taken one more step in that direction.

The things that now stands out in my mind about Cal was (1) good intellectual discussion not available in Blythe, (2) Marge, (3) the wonderment of college sports (I had been recruited to the Cal crew to be a coxswain due to my 100 lb. frame and I spent four years with the crew), and (4) Marge.

When you are arriving from the desert, as I did, one does not have any background in the elegant but grueling sport of team rowing, or crew, as we call it. Even given that Blythe lies on the banks of the Colorado River, the idea of going into what was then a fast-flowing and treacherous current with only a set of oars would be crazy. So when I was stopped in the freshman registration line by a couple of six-foot-plus guys wearing varsity letterman jackets who asked me if I wanted to be a coxswain, I thought they were kidding. However, after asking some questions at my frat house, I was informed that rowing was a big deal at Cal (where three Olympic champion crews had been produced under the guidance of Ky Ebright), and I would be lucky to be part of that.

I let the crew office know I was interested, and they signed me up. As it turned out, my next four years was devoted to that year-round sport. (We practiced from the time school started in the fall until Thanksgiving, restarting again in late January to get ready for the spring competition.) Every late afternoon and some Saturdays were always spent at the California Boathouse on the Oakland Estuary, no matter the weather, leaving little time for studies, fun, and just being a college kid.

I eventually lettered in the crew, twice occupying the coxswain's seat for a couple of important races. Looking back now, after sixty-five years of retrospection, I often wonder if I did all I could have done as a team leader. Sure, I could steer the 62' long, 18" wide shell smoothly on a straight course under any kind of weather or race conditions while yelling out corrections to the oarsmen and plotting strategy, but to this day, I am not sure I did enough as a leader. I will probably go to my grave with that question unanswered. Nevertheless, I am certain that having to perform precise activities while under a lot of stress probably was a good training for the flying situations I encountered later.

I had a big distraction in those years, and her name was Marge.

I first met Marge while shopping on Telegraph Avenue. She was coming out of a drugstore, and boy, was she a sight. She was dressed in a white nurse's uniform that clung to her body and showed some great legs. She was sporting a ponytail, had deep brown eyes and a big smile. I was with a fraternity brother who bet me she would not talk to me if I approached her. So being in a competitive spirit, I stopped her and asked her name. My buddy, who was a ladies' man, had expected me to strike out and then he would step in and take over.

It did not happen that way. She responded with a big smile, and that was the beginning of a sixty-four-year relationship. My buddy, sort of jealous, had later tried to date her, but she did not like his smug, big-city approach (he was from San Francisco), and in fact, he sort of frightened her, as I later learned.

Marge was a Midwestern girl, born in St. Paul and brought up in Elkhart, Indiana. She was part German, part French, and part Chippewa, and it all showed. Her mother had walked out on her and her sister when they were preteens, and she was then raised by her working father and the mother of her best friend, Ruth Ann, and her mother who lived next door. They communicated until her death.

Even when I say that her native American characteristics showed, neither I and, surprisingly, Marge knew why anything about her Indian heritage at that time.

Mabel, her mother, was half native American Indian and was, it seemed, born on the reservation belonging to the White Earth Band of the Chippewa Nation, her father being a French-Canadian trader. Her birth certificate showed she was born in St. Paul, but as it turns out, if you were born on the reservation, your birth certificate would show "St. Paul" as the place of birth. Like many Native Americans of the period, her mother hid her heritage. It was not until several years after we left the Air Force that she found out about her heritage.

One day, while living in Martinez, she got a check from the Bureau of Indian Affairs without any accompanying explanation. It was not a large check (around $400), but what questions it raised!. Why would she get this? She called her mother in Los Angeles, where she had settled down after leaving Elkhart, and then ensued a two-hour discussion about the whole story of her heritage.

My family did not like her from the start. Too good looking for me (I still weighed about 105 lb. and still had ears that stuck out), so she must have had bad reasons for enticing me. I decided then that maybe going into the Air Force after graduation was a good solution for the time being, so when I graduated (I missed the ceremony since I was in the east with the Cal crew and therefore did not have to put up with family upset) and after a few months of living together in my apartment in Berkeley, we got married.

I can't imagine what life would have been like without her. Notwithstanding the support I received from her in the Air Force, her help and inspiration blossomed when we returned to Martinez.

She went out of way to improve relations with my family and involved herself with community projects that earned her many friendships in a short time. She was a natural to be drawn into politics. The Martinez we worked in was a middle class, labor-oriented environment, and Marge soon become the treasurer for the election of a young congressman named George Miller, who went on to have a long career in the House of Representatives, influencing a large block of legislation. Marge went to work on his staff and became district rep, putting her in charge of the district office. She was twice elected to be chairperson of the county Democratic Central Committee.

She left her post with the congressman to help me start my real estate office, and she became a licensed salesperson and also managed the office, all the while being a concerned mother to our son, Mark, and daughter, Marissa.

It is hard to overestimate what Marge was all about. She had the looks of a movie star and the soul of a saint. Everything she touched seemed to be better in some way. As she matured, so did her looks, never losing that touch she was given at birth. She always went in the direction she needed to take to help me or her children or someone she touched. During my Air Force years, I could find her shining my shoes at night, which I never wanted to do, but she didn't think it was good for me. I refused to shine them as a matter of point. I was risking my life for the country every day, I felt, so why did I have to do it with shined shoes? She continued to do this for the rest of our marriage, even after the Air Force.

To Marge, home and family came first. The last thing you would say about her was that she was an extrovert, but when presented with challenges that she believed in, she always rose to meet the challenge. She played the piano, and we had one in our living room, but she would not play with anyone around (even me). She was afraid of speaking from a podium, but when she had to, she did a marvelous and compelling job. When waiting to compete in a national competition with her dog, her knees would shake, and she suffered from stage fright. But when her time came to perform before judges and a stand full of spectators, she made it look smooth and graceful and brought cheers and applause from the spectators.

She had a strong inner drive to travel and see the world, so with some good friends and neighbors, she promoted trips all over the world, sometimes with our friends and sometimes not. Her goal was to be on every continent and to visit the North Pole. We accomplished everything except the North Pole thing. I kept telling her that there was nothing there. I had flown over it while in the Air Force, and believe me, unlike Antarctica, there was no land there. Trips to USSR (when it still was the USSR), the Amazon, the Antarctic Peninsula, Cape Town, Beijing, Paris, Istanbul, and others I shall not bother with here, were all handled by her with grace and energy, making everyone else feel good.

Thanks to Marge, we always had a dog. She had a nice bond with animals, especially dogs, and except for a few times when we were younger and the logistics were not right, we had a dog. When she was in her late sixties, she decided to buy a female border collie pup from a ranch in a nearby town. The price was $150, and the dog's name was Chellie, and Chellie changed all our lives.

A friend told her that we lived within a quarter mile from a topnotch agility trainer, and she should try her luck getting involved with that sport. Marge contacted her and started lessons. Sharon, the trainer, demanded excellence from her students, and neighbors were no exception. She was hard on Marge at the start, and Marge would come home with tears after a tough session.

But things changed. With the same grace and competence that Marge had displayed in all the other projects she had undertaken, she not only mastered the sport, but with her great dog, Chellie, rose to the top of the competitive cream. She got into doing the agility course using larger and larger distances between her and the dog. I used to watch spectators using such phrases as "oh my god" and "wow" when watching her and Chellie perform a distance event, where she stood behind a line and directed Chellie through the course with verbal and hand signals.

We (I got into it also) competed in an association (North American Dog Agility Council) that had a an annual championship trial that included qualified participants from all over the US and Canada and included a special division on distance handling. In 2007, she won the title for her division and indeed was the star of that part of the sport. She went on in subsequent years to set high marks and win other trophies in that sport. But her biggest contribution, I believe, was the way she interacted with her fellow competitors, helping anyone she could, encouraging handlers while making friends. Above all, she was a role model.

She was, in her seventies, still planning a trip to the North Pole when she was diagnosed with lung cancer and passed away in the summer of 2018. She was mourned by many, and the Agility Association honored her at the fall championship.

Like everything else she did, she left her mark. Next to Mr. Mclaughlin, who we will talk more about soon, she also taught me some great lessons.

Probably one of the most significant and stressful times of my life was my senior year at Berkeley. I was seriously involved with Marge, who had become the most important thing in my life, mentally preparing to enter the Air Force, as I was required to do after graduation, completing my studies, and participating in rowing practice and competition. Both sides of my family did not like my involvement with Marge, first because she was not of the same religion, and second because she was independent. It was especially disappointing that my aunt Roz, who up to then had been a guiding light (and much like a mother), did not like her.

I came down with mono in the spring of 1956 and spent a week in the campus hospital. I got out just in time to join the California crew annual trip to the East Coast for the national collegiate championships. Due to my illness and then my trip, I was not able to take my final exams, but the university said my midterms were good enough to carry me. Due to the trip east, I could not participate in graduation ceremonies. My diploma was mailed to me.

I decided on the trip east that I was going to marry Marge.

Entering the Air Force worked into that plan well, since getting away from family and being with Marge was a good combination of events.

We were lovers and partners for the next sixty-two years, until she passed away due to lung cancer.

My aunt Roz, who, up until her death, was still like a mother to me, and Marge became close friends. When she became ill while living alone in LA and needed help, Marge drove down to LA, put her in the car, and brought her to our home, where she nursed her back to health and then helped her relocate to an apartment in San Francisco. There she spent several happy years until she died of liver cancer while in Marge's arms.

Marge and I decided to elope, so with two of my fraternity brothers coming along for support, we flew to Reno and got married. Marge moved into my apartment for a short time, but we kept the marriage secret from our families until I was called up to report to Lackland Air Force Base to start my required tour. Marge's dad took it well and wished us good luck. My family did not quite respond that way at the time, but then we were, for all practical purposes, hitting the road.

Our time in the Air Force and being away from our families turned out to be a great fix. As time went on and my family got to know Marge, they took a different view of our marriage. Marge's father, who was, for all practical purposes, her only family, was good with the marriage from the start.

The Air Force

In the fall of 1956, with so much still ahead for us, we started our first adventure, and we headed to San Antonio, with me as a young lieutenant and ready to start a new phase of our lives.

Lackland Air Force Base in San Antonio was an induction spot for the western US. There you bought your uniform, learned how to wear it and what to expect as an officer in the military. The only thing I remember about Lackland was the struggle I had in passing the flight physical due to my light weight and apparent lack of depth perception, which was required as a pilot. For two weeks, I ate bananas and drank milk and anything else that would put five pounds on me. The Air Force had a standard test in its flight physical procedure that involved lining up two side-by-side pegs while sitting on a stool, maybe ten feet away, and using two cords, one for each peg, that were not of equal length. It is tricky, and you really had to have good depth perception to succeed. I could not do it, and in fact, I had a depth perception problem, which I still have. I could not line up two pegs in front of me with cords I had in my hands. I could not do that today. The airman testing me (after several return trips to try to pass the tests) left the room to go to the bathroom, and I went over to table where the pegs were and figured out where the cords should be for the pegs to be lined up. When he returned, I had the test set up so I could not fail. I was almost sure he had done that on purpose to give me a chance to pass my flight physical. Although I had a depth perception problem, I had learned to handle it in flying, where you need that ability for landing a plane, by not looking directly at the runway.

Today, when I pull into a parking spot, I often stop three feet short of the front end.

I passed the weight test with some help from another airman who put his foot on the scale. Alright, I was ready to go to flight school. The interesting thing was that it was so hard to pass your first flight physical, but once you had your wings and were in an operational unit, just try to flunk a flight physical! The second thing I remember about Lackland was the thrill Marge got every time I drove through the main gate and the sentry saluted me because I was wearing a second lieutenant's bars on my shoulder. The first time she made me go out again so I could come back in and he had to do it again. She was tickled.

Having finally passed my tests, I was assigned to a flight school at Bartow Air Base, just outside Winter Haven, Florida, and off we went to Florida.

The assignment to Bartow Air Base was exciting, since it was just outside Winter Haven, Florida, a well-known (at the time) seasonal visitor destination with Cypress Gardens and their water ski show, a famous attraction. One of the first thing we did was to visit Cypress Gardens.

Bartow Air Base was first built as an Army Air Corps facility in the early stages of WWII and later transferred to the Air Force, who operated it as a contract training facility where the instructors were ex-Air Force or Army Air Corps pilots who had left the service for reasons that were out of their hands but were qualified to be civilian instructors. Many of them were not happy about how their lives went, and it showed sometimes. But more about that later.

We found a small duplex apartment with a yard so that Marge could get a dog. We always, except for short periods, had some type of dog. This time it was a Boxer called Lady, and she shared the small bed with us so it got crowded. Our landlord, as he quickly announced, was also our personal bootlegger, and we should get all our liquor through him. Polk County was a dry county, and apparently that was a local real estate custom.

I started my training at Bartow and met my instructor (who would have a much bigger impact on my Air Force career than I would have thought at the time). His name was Mclaughin, and we called him Mr. Mclaughin. He had, as best I could make out, been one of those WWII pilots who, as an enlisted soldier in the Army, was sent to flight school, earned an officer's commission because he became a fighter pilot, and flew P-51s (later called F 51s) Mustang fighters in France and Germany, with hours of giving ground support to troops, strafing German supply trains, and engaging enemy fighters. He wore a fight suit with the collar turned up, a baseball cap slightly tilted forward, and if he was not wearing his leather flying gloves, he was a carrying them or had them sticking out of a pocket. He was right out of central casting (as we say).

From what I could tell, he left the Army after WWII, was called back for the Korean conflict, but after that was over, he was not qualified to remain in the service due to lack of education. This happened to lots of pilots in that era, and it affected their lives very negatively.

The normal working day at Bartow was that half the pilot class had ground school in the morning and had a flying period in the afternoon, where they got instruction periods of one hour with, or later without, their instructor. The next month, the scheduled was flipped. The flying period started with a sit-down briefing from our instructor at a table in the flight operations room. It accommodated the instructor and his three normally assigned students that he was responsible for. Due to the need for pilots in the Air Force at the time, sometimes a fourth pilot was assigned to an instructor. That created stress for the instructor since there was three one-hour flying periods and if there was a fourth student, then the instructor would have to work overtime. Mr. Mclaughlin let it be known from the start that he did not like having four students and it would be down to three real quick. Someone would wash out. I was determined and confident it would not be me. Two of the other students were captains that were navigators with lots of time in the B66 in Korea and had a lot in common with Mac (as we called him for short among ourselves), so they were not going anywhere real soon. That left me and a second lieutenant from Texas A&M that was my contemporary. He was a nice guy but had no flying background and seemed a little timid about the prospect.

A while into the program, Mac, in a moment of irritation, told me that he did not particularly like me, an ROTC student from Berkeley, but I was safe from losing my place at the table because I did not make any trouble for him or extra work. Great.

The T-34 trainer, which had a tricycle landing gear and straight tail, was derived from the Beechcraft Bonanza, which has the highly identifiable V tail, but much more of a stable and maneuverable aircraft. I have flown both, and the T-34 was a sweet plane. It had a tricycle retractable nose gear that the Air Force thought was much more appropriate as opposed to the trail draggers that had previously been the primary teaching aircraft, such as the famous T-6. Since the jets we would eventually be flying had tricycle landing gear, this would be understandable. It handled easily, was stable in flight, and capable of acrobatics. The pilots sat in tandem and had, as was normal for that type of arrangement, mechanically linked control sticks so that when one moves, the other does also. Communications between pilots was by intercom and through the headsets worn by the pilots. The noise level and seating discouraged normal conversation. There was also a "mixer box" beside each pilot so that the desired input to the earphones, either VHF, UHF, or intercom could be selected with the toggle switches.

Then there was the mystery of the ring. Before we started our flight program, Mac took myself and the other second lieutenant aside to lecture us about our wedding rings.

"You cannot fly with wedding rings on," he said. "They are very dangerous in the event that you have to bail out." He had a very serious look about him. "If you have to bail out, you will climb out on the wing on the left side of the cockpit and holding on to the edge of the cockpit with your left hand, work your way back on the wing towards the trailing edge and, when you are ready, let go with your left hand and jump over the flaps head down into the sky. In that procedure, your left hand would slide over the surface of the plane, which is filled with rows of rivets. Your wedding ring could possibly, while sliding over the side of the fuselage, catch on a rivet and because of the force, tear your finger off."

This all seemed quite plausible, as I could see myself diving into space with my hand dripping blood and maybe unable to pull the rip cord.

Okay, I'm in.

When I got home that night, I explained to Marge how I had to take my ring off. She looked at me in a way I would come to know well over the next sixty-two years. "I'm not kidding! We are all doing the same thing." By morning, she was okay with it.

Safety first.

It became so automatic that I did not think about it for a couple of years until I got into an operational unit.

Our first dual flights let Mac know I could handle an airplane. There was a required lesson plan prior to soloing, and if you were not ready to solo at the completion of the plans, you might be in trouble. Mac made it be known right away that we flew his way and not mine. All maneuvers were crisp, and he did not like wasting time being in level flight. There were maneuvers to practice, always.

He flew with a chip on his shoulder, just like he presented himself at the briefing table. He taught his students, at least those who survived the program, to fly the same way. Many times later on, that attitude made a big difference in bad situations and, I would say, probably saved my life as well as the crew's.

One of the required maneuvers to learn and demonstrate was the two-turn spin, something that was not a thing students looked forward to. It was taught for two reasons, first to teach you how to get out of one, the other to test your orientation in critical phases of flight when disorientation was on top of you. To enter a spin, you pulled the throttle back to cut power, lifted the nose until it stalled, kicked the rudder (I preferred the right), and the plane would fall off into an uncontrolled spin. The requirement was for the student pilot to keep the plane in the spin for two full turns by holding the stick back and rudder in before pushing the stick forward, hitting the opposite rudder, letting the plane gain speed and the spin will stop. Then you can level the plane off, add power, and start a climb. The toughest part was to keep your orientation so as to stop the spin exactly at two turns. One did this by picking out a landmark on the ground that was in front of you and was prominent enough so you would not lose sight of it. Go by it once, then kick the rudder when it came around again. It happened fast.

Mac liked my spins, and a couple of days later, we were practicing landings (doing touch-and-gos) when Mac complained over the intercom that he was sick of flying with me and to pull over to the side of the runway and let him out. He was sending me solo and wanted to make sure I was wearing my chip. I was. The requirement was to do three acceptable landings while Mac watched from an observation post at the end of the runway along with his supervisor. It was an important test, not only to do it successfully but smoothly. Like most planes, the T-34 required flats to be lowered to a certain point on final to land safely at a reasonable speed. Not to use flaps was for emergencies and considered dangerous for new pilots, as was a no-flap takeoff.

My first landing was by the book, but on the second landing, I forgot to lower the flaps. Nevertheless, it was a smooth landing and a smooth no-flap takeoff. After my third landing, I pulled over to let Mac climb back in the cockpit. The first thing he said was, "You just had to show off with the no-flap landing, didn't you?" I was not about to admit it was a mistake and just smiled.

Although I did not realize it at the time, that was probably the first event that would lead me to end up with a training report as a "smart aleck."

CHAPTER 5

The T-28 and Leaving Bartow

The Air Force, when I entered pilot training, had a policy of grading student pilots during their training from the start to getting their wings so as to establish a class graduating order like the academies did. You got to choose from a list of the available pilot assignments according to your class position so that the top of the class got first pick, etc. The idea was to finish high enough to get a good assignment. Flying and ground school counted about evenly, but a 10 percent area of grading was how your wife contributed to Air Force life. Marge picked up that from day 1 at Bartow and jumped in to do her part, just like she would do throughout our marriage. She participated in everything she could, helping out wherever she could, and even wrote a column for the base newspaper.

It would be hard to explain today why a spouse's activity should be part of your flying grade, but it was a good thing for Marge, giving her a reason to associate with other wives that were a little older than her and with college educations, which she did not have. It was a growing experience for her, and she ate it up.

Meanwhile, I had moved on from the T-34 to the more sophisticated T-28. Produced by North American Aviation, the 800 hp trainer had a cockpit setup similar to a single-engine jet so as to ease transition for pilots moving to single-engine jets. They were faster, more complicated, and not as forgiving as a T-34. The Navy had the same plane with a more powerful engine, and it was used in Vietnam for close ground support. My relationship with Mac continued to be spotty. We sometimes hit it off and then we clashed. When I could not take any more of his chiding over the intercom, I would shut it off by closing the toggle switch so that I could not hear him in my head and then point to my ears and shake my head. He would respond by grabbing the stick, which was mechanically linked to mine, putting the plane in a stall position so that the stick was slack and then beat the inside of my legs in order to make a point.

Then I turned on my headset.

Once, I caught him in my rearview mirror bending over to write notes on his ever-present knee pad while we were in a steep descent with a lot speed. I pulled sharply back on the stick in order to create a strong gravity pull (g's as it is called) of about 3 g's, thereby making it hard if not impossible to straighten up. He was less than happy about that. When the exercise was over, he took control of the plane, stalled it, and beat my legs with the control stick. I always thought he encouraged this type of activity, but he did not seem to like it when I did it.

When someone in the class had to fly a check ride with an Air Force military check pilot who was testing the quality of training, Mac sent me. Getting even? Maybe, or maybe he needed someone with a chip so as not to be intimidated. I will never know for sure. But I passed.

The remainder of the program centered on aerobatics, instrument training, and cross-country trips. Graduation from primary flying school was pretty certain. We had to choose between going to the next step, basic flying school for single-engine (fighter pilot) training or multi-engine school. I had been encouraged by Mac several times to be a fighter pilot. He wanted all his students to be fighter pilots like him. He considered it a slap in the face if a qualified student went to multi-engine training. When he asked me, I would indicate "fighter pilot all the way."

That was not going to happen. My son, Mark, had been born while we were in Winter Haven, and the single-engine bases were all in the boondocks. No housing or other facilities one would want. So I picked multi-flying, and we were picked to go to Goodfellow AFB at San Angelo, Texas. I thought I was through with Mac, but that was not to be the case. The chip he wore had infected me, although it would take a couple of years to understand that. It was mentioned to me some years later by crew members that my personality changed when I strapped in. I was normally a person with a more quiet, friendly personality when not in the cockpit. A couple of years later, while undergoing transition training to KC-135s (SAC's new jet-powered tanker), my instructor, when practicing in-flight emergency procedures, announced, "When I pull an emergency procedure on you, the first thing I want to hear from you is, 'Goddamned son of a bitch,' and loudly. Then you can start your emergency procedure. The idea was to put a "chip" on your shoulder so that you were in the mood to not let the airplane push you around. If you did that, you were in danger. Things happen fast in a jet. Better to be in the mood to win. I always practiced that procedure and found it more than useful, maybe life-saving.

Mac was on the right track. I tried to find him some years later to thank him, but failed.

Goodfellow was a real military facility, with taps being played in the evening while the flag was lowered, and on Friday afternoon, a fly-over of three B-25s in formation on a low-level path right over the base flagpole. It was a moving sight. I never got tired of seeing that or the B-25s lined the flight line. Famous for the flight led by Doolittle from a carrier to bomb Tokyo early in WWII, the B-25 was emblematic of WWII, I always thought, so the thought of flying one in training was exciting. Marge and I settled in easily, and we really liked San Angelo.

The North American B-25 Mitchell came into use about 1940 and was considered one of the most useable aircraft in WWII. It was used for many tasks. It had a top speed of about three hundred miles per hour, a very sturdy landing gear that was designed for the aircraft to land on surface rougher than a runway. The armor and guns had been removed for pilot training, but still I found it to require a good deal of effort to handle the controls. I barely had the strength, it seemed, to pull the nose up for landing in a smooth manner without rolling in a lot of nose up trim on final and holding the yolk forward, so that when it became time to raise the nose for landing attitude, I mostly relaxed pressure forward. That allowed me to make a smooth and controlled pitch change. I was not alone in that observation as my flight of fellow students got together and bought dark brown "truck driver" type of caps that we all liked to wear when we could. We were one of the last flight classes to fly the B-25, as it was retired soon after. Looking back, I was happy to have a chance to accrue hours in that aircraft.

One of the first events that occurred at the base was a demonstration put on to show how the B-25 was able to take off from an aircraft carrier in the Pacific loaded with bombs and other armaments in order to perform the famous attack on Japan. This was traditional and a must for all student pilots and their wives.

There was an auxiliary landing strip about ten miles from the main base. This was used for student pilots, with or without instructors, to go out and practice landings, mainly touch-and-gos, while not disturbing the air traffic at the main base. These are called bounce strips. This bounce strip was located in an area of sandy high desert and was fenced off with a typical barbed wire fence, as was used in west Texas.

Before we got into our training program, there was a "ceremony" required for pilots and their wives.

All the wives were bused to the bounce strips and lined up along the runway to watch. An area equivalent to the length of the carrier deck on the USS *Hornet* was marked off with tape. (Boy, was it short!) Each B-25, with its full complement of instructor and student pilots, lined up at the beginning of the marked-off area, ran its engines up to full power while holding the plane with its brakes, and when a flag was waved by an airman beside the runway (for additional drama), the instructor pilot on the plane released the brakes, and the plane lunged forward. My teeth were clenched. It felt scary. We got to the marker at the end of the marked-off area, and the pilot lowered full flaps. The plane wobbled into the air, hanging on its props and shuddering, as happens prior to a stall. Scary. Gradually the plane picked up speed, the nose was lowered, the gear retracted, and off we went. While we were flying planes that had been lightened by taking away armor and bombs, the planes taking off from the carrier had, at least, a headwind of some kind due to the forward motion of the carrier. We had no wind.

When we went around, landed, and greeted our wives, Marge's comment was, "That looked like fun."

Okay.

My first day on the flight line was a shock. The students were split into groups of three, so that we all flew with the instructor at the same time. Since the plane had two seats behind the pilots, we could rotate seats as the instructor wanted. When we flew solo, two students would take the plane, one being pilot and one the copilot.

We were ready to start, and our instructor walked up. He looked like a linebacker for a football team with an attitude to match. He was carrying a big stick. When I asked what the stick was for, he looked at me with a frown and said, "It's for you."

I was confused. I was not going to fight him. I weighed about 120 lb. He weighed, I would guess, 230 lb. Glaring at me, he said, "I read your training report. You are not going to pull any stuff on me." Now I was upset. Mac had gotten even with me for going to multi-engines, I figured. He went on, "If you try to pull any cute tricks while flying with me, I am going to beat your hands with this stick."

Later I found out the specifics of what he was talking about.

Student pilots in multi-engine school, as I mentioned, were paired off in twos so that during solo flights, one would be pilot and one copilot in an alternate manner, so that we could learn the position of both and keep an eye on each other. We studied together, and in the beginning, Fred, my partner, and I would gather in my kitchen, sitting side by side in kitchen chairs arranged like in the airplane while Marge held a copy of the flight checklist, that we all carried on flights, as we, in turns, called out emergency procedures that we were required to memorize prior to solo flight, while Marge followed along on the list to make sure we were right.

The most important procedure to know was the single-engine procedure. One of the most serious emergencies was the loss of an engine, which not only caused loss of power, but more seriously, the loss of directional control in critical phases of flight. There was a twenty-five step procedure, I remember, and among the first that had to be memorized were the immediate ones to gain directional control. "Rudder, RPM, mixture, throttle, feather, trim rudder," were, as I remember, absolutely to be done right and in that order. Later, steps in the procedure could be read from the checklist after control was restored. We practiced that maneuver over and over both on the ground and in the air. Feathering, by the way, was a mechanical procedure that turned the propeller blades parallel with the airstream to eliminate the huge drag created by a dead propeller with its flat blades facing the airstream. This is a procedure that all multi-engine pilots in propeller-driven planes know all too well.

As it turned out, one of the favorite tricks of smart-aleck students like me was during single-engine practice in flight, when the instructor pulled the throttle back to idle on either the port or starboard engine to simulate an engine failure, the smart-aleck student would feather the other engine, therefore creating a sudden quiet that upset not only the instructor but everyone on board and required immediate action to restore some power.

"If you do that, Lieutenant, I am going to break your hand, the one used to push the feathering button, just to start." I never did that nor even thought about doing it, as the thought was scary to me also.

After several flights, my instructor decided that I was not a threat to his safety and really quite reasonable. We started to get along, and he quit carrying his stick.

B-25 school was different from Bartow, where our instructors were older, seasoned pilots with superior attitudes, but rather lieutenants like us that had gotten their wings maybe only a couple of years ahead of us, except for the flight commander and the squadron commander. They were more like Bartow and were captains that had been in grade for some time.

After some weeks of positive progress among myself and our class, Christmas season arrived, and the flight commander decided to have a Christmas party that required the most formal uniform we could find and bow ties. Everyone drank too much, and somewhere in the evening, my flight commander decided to get a little fresh with Marge when I was not around. He played the piano and considered himself the life of the party. Marge, being Marge, waited until he sat himself down to play the piano and then turned a bowl of peanut dip upside down on his head while he was playing the piano. I had been out of the room, and when I returned to see what had happened, I grabbed Marge and we got out of there.

Although it was certainly not her fault and would have been applauded in today's #MeToo world, it was different in those days and those circumstances.

The next day, I found out I had been scheduled for a check ride to see if I was a safe and capable pilot. This was with the squadron commander I was to fly with, and he was not too friendly.

We took off, with me in the pilot's seat and the captain in the right seat, where instructors usually sit. He ordered me to climb out and do some turns, then of course, pulled back on a throttle to initiate the single-engine maneuver. This was always a maneuver that could always be criticized by an instructor. There was a lot to do in a short time, and that made for wide possibility to criticize the student, or fail him, if so included.

I nailed it. No room for criticism.

We headed to the bounce strip. A standard, non-instrument VFR approach was to fly up to the runway in the direction of landing, about eight hundred to one thousand feet above the runway. Then when you crossed the runway, you made a sharp, descending 360-degree turn so that you rolled out on final approach in line with the runway and at the proper elevation for the final approach and landing. The B-25 approach we used was a tactical one, meant for being in or near a combat zone, so you wanted to have minimum exposure to enemy fire, therefore the sharp descending turn to a position where you flew a low, flat approach to the runway on final approach, just clearing the barbed wire fence at the edge of the field and the runway.

My approach was good. I was lined up for landing and about to cross the fence at the field boundary, flaps and gear down and ready for landing. Suddenly I felt the plane start to sink.

The flap control was located between the pilots so that either could operate it, and below the level of the pilot's seats near the floor of the cockpit. The captain had slipped his left hand down and pulled up the flap handle, thereby causing the plane to lose lift. I noticed, out of the corner of my eye, that his left arm was lowered toward the flap handle. I reacted quickly, knocking his left arm sharply aside from flap handle, put the flaps back down, and added full power. By that time, we were too low not to touch down on the desert, and the wire fence was in front of us and between us and the runway, so I let it touch down, then pulled sharply back on the yolk and bounced over the wire fence, then touched the plane down on the apron in front of the runway and taxied up to the runway with no harm to the aircraft.

The check pilot just looked at me and sort of nodded. I had passed. I will never really know if the sneak-up-the-flap thing was used with other students, or was it just meant for me?

After that, everything was cool with the flight instructors, and I got my wings.

As I mentioned, there was a procedure in the Air Force that new pilots could pick from the available assignments at the time of graduation according to how they ranked in the graduation of the class. Notwithstanding some of my earlier instances in clashing with my instructors, I finished in the top 20 percent of the class, mostly due to my high grades in ground school, where I got along with instructors. I was thrilled. We were going to get a good assignment, hopefully where housing was good and the weather tolerable.

Surprise! There was a letter on the bulletin board, that announced that due to its needs, SAC was going to take the top 25 percent of the class and the rest could pick their assignments from the list. General Le May, SAC commander in chief, told the Air Force that he was tired of getting the bottom of the class and he needed better and more qualified pilots. SAC had a bad reputation among the student pilots, since an assignment in SAC meant low flying hours due to time on alert, lots of pressure, lots of time away from your family, and a good chance of an isolated base in a cold climate.

The students who went to single-engine school ended up with the same situation.

A lot of the pilots who flew B-25s were assigned to KC-97 tankers, and the most of the ones that went to single engine (and flew the T-33 jet trainer) went to the B-47. I was assigned to KC-97s at Little Rock AFB after a six-week training session at Randolph AFB in San Antonio.

CHAPTER 6

Little Rock

The Strategic Air Command had naturally evolved from the Bomber Command of the Army Air Force and the demonstrated success that strategic bombing had on the war effort. In the fifties and sixties, the US was rightly concerned about the problem of protecting the homeland from a growing Soviet potential to attack us by flying longer-range bombers over the pole. We established the DEW Line (Distant Early Warning), which stretched from Thule Air Base in Greenland across far northern Canada to Alaska. Huge radar antennas could virtually see over the pole and thereby detect aircraft heading our way from the Soviet Union in time to take defensive action, one of which was the capability of immediate nuclear retaliation by the long-range US bombers going back over the polar area. There was a second radar waning line established across mid-Canada as a backup. Some of the holes in the screen were patrolled by multi-engine planes flying continually over the North Atlantic and North Pacific.

Eventually, intercontinental ballistic missiles (ICBMs) would become the major weapon of deterrence, but when I was in SAC, it was clear to us that we (SAC) were the major defense against aggression by the Soviet by virtue of the fear of retaliation.

The B-47, developed by Boeing as a medium-range bomber, was the first step in the retaliation theat. This six-engine aircraft was to hold the line until the B-52, then under development, would come on line to replace the B-47, which as we eventually learned, had faults as an aircraft and a shorter range than desired. The B-47 had some warts, such as a flexible wing that due to metal fatigue (I had been told), would crack in flight, thereby causing in-flight disasters and resultant crashes, even while carrying nuclear weapons. I read that in those days, the Soviet Union did not have the capability to drop a nuclear weapon on the US, but we did.

Air refueling made it a long-range bomber.

This was the aircraft used in the then popular movie *Strategic Air Command* with Jimmy Stewart, that at the time became the face of SAC to me and my friends. However, it, like its successor, the B-52 needed in-flight refueling to make it to its potential targets and return. Curtis Le May, working under President Eisenhower, as first SAC commander and then the chief of the Air Force was overseeing the development of a jet-powered tanker aircraft to match the jet-powered bombers. But meanwhile, the four-engine propeller-driven C-97 was to be configured as SAC's in-flight refueler and became the KC-97. Together, this pair of aircraft would be our major symbol of deterrence, our then stated plan of defense.

There were problems in matching a jet-powered, sweptwing bomber with a propeller-driven straight-wing transport that had its own warts. The KC had to push itself to keep up the speed needed to "mate" in flight with the B-47.

More on that later. These were things I was to learn about, starting with my arrival at Little Rock AFB. I remember reading the sign at the front gate and found everywhere there was a SAC base: Peace Is Our Profession.

Marge and I, at first, dreaded our assignment to Little Rock. We had been watching the evening news, which had been headlining the confrontation taking place at Little Rock's Central High School when nine Afro-American students tried to enroll, and Governor Orval Faubus blocked the door. Eisenhower was sending one thousand paratroopers to keep the peace. The newspaper pictures looked like the whole town was in the streets. For a graduate of University of California, this was not looking like a pleasant assignment.

However, we loved Little Rock. Built on the banks of the Arkansas River, which at that point, is a dividing line between the level topography of southern Arkansas and the beginning of the Ozarks, Little Rock AFB was a new base, built I believe for SAC. It was located about twenty minutes north of Little Rock next to a town called Jacksonville We at first moved into a fourplex in North Little Rock with some other aircrew families. This was temporary, we were told, since SAC was building new housing on the base for families in order to help morale. Families did not like SAC, and retention was low. They needed aircrew members and pilots who would stay and do their job. The housing construction was part of that plan, and indeed in a few months, we moved into a new single family dwelling that we got to pick out.

The weather was generally bearable. The people were friendly, the countryside pretty, and prices were low. There was a restaurant in downtown Little Rock that served great steaks and huge baked potatoes with like a quarter pound of butter on it at a really reasonable price. We went there whenever we got a night out.

I had become friends with a captain who was transferred to Tankers from a plush assignment in Houston flying navigators around in navigator school. SAC wanted qualified pilots. His name was John Purdy. His wife's name was Ruth, and the four of us became good friends right away, and our friendship has lasted since then. Years after we had all left the Air Force, we kept in touch, especially with Ruth, who had settled in Cheyenne after she and John got a divorce. For many years, Marge and I traveled to Gillette, Wyoming, for a competition, and we always stayed overnight at Ruth's on the way. Marge insisted.

I met John at Randolph Field. He had about three thousand hours, and I had just got my wings. We were put together to train in KC-97s. When we picked out a house at the base, they moved in a couple of doors away. We had hoped to fly together, but that was not to happen for a while.

John and I reported together to our assigned outfit, the Seventieth Air Refueling Squadron, which was part of the Seventieth Strategic Recon Wing, a B-47 outfit that was currently being used to train B-47 pilots for aerial refueling. The headquarters was located on the base flight line behind the barbed-wire topped chain-link fence that separates the base proper from the classified area requiring a badge to access. It was in a one-story not-too-impressive building, but behind it were rows of KC-97s, and a little farther away were rows of B-47s. To me, it was an awesome sight. Once inside, we were sent to the operations office to produce our orders and get briefed on our jobs. I was told the squadron commander wanted to see me.

A little surprised, I was ushered into his office by the operations officer, who would also be in the meeting. After saluting, I was asked to sit down. The commander produced a file and glanced into it. "Lieutenant, this is your training report, and it says that you can fly but you have an attitude problem and you like to challenge authority."

Great, I thought, *Mac is still getting even with me. Now what?*

They looked at me sternly. Finally, the CO spoke. "You are just what we were looking for. Our squadron has several aircraft commanders [pilots who have enough flight hours and time in grade to be assigned to command the crew] that are close to retirement, not too motivated to fly anymore, and in some cases need some help in operating the aircraft and/or completing the mission. You could be of great help flying with them."

I was relieved. I had a place here after all.

The problem was one that I would guess existed throughout the KC-97 fleet. Aircrew members, especially pilots and flight engineers were largely people who had served in WWII, released, and then recalled for the Korean War. They had not much to look forward to except good food, whiskey, and retirement. They were stuck in grade, due to lack of a college degree. Like the instructors in Bartow, President Eisenhower's defense spending policies had not been kind to them. No wonder General Le May was looking for fresh blood. The strategic assignment SAC had taken on needed to keep life in the tanker operation.

I was not going to fly with John for some time.

The KC-97 was developed in the forties by Boeing, as I understand it, both as a military useable aircraft, having evolved from the B-29 Superfortress in several ways, and it was useable by airlines to carry passengers and cargo along the East Coast. It was one of the first passenger aircraft to have a pressurized cabin, and that made it useable by SAC in its modified role as an aerial refueling source. It could be said that it was a B-29, fattened up, lengthened, and put on a tricycle landing gear. It was powered with four Pratt & Whitney R 4360 radial engines, each developing over 3,000 hp. Each engine had twenty-eight cylinders and two spark plugs per cylinder. It was, as I understand, the last conventional piston-driven aircraft engine that came from mass production. It was the end of the line for gasoline-powered engines in aircraft on a production level. And I would be quick to agree, having seen them being nursed by flight engineers to do a job that was "over their piston rings," as one might say. The engines used a huge amount of oil, and propellers that constantly needed to be resynched with each other during flight or risk damaging vibrations that could possibly cause the destruction of the aircraft.

I recall that each engine had its own oil tank (reservoir) that was supplied by a central oil tank through lines controlled by the flight engineer, who could monitor the oil level in each engine, and using a built-in pump, transfer oil to each engine as needed. In addition to the central oil tank, we carried, on long flights, a fifty-gallon drum of oil strapped to the upper level deck next to a port that could be opened in flight and oil pumped in through a short hose, using a hand crank such as one might have seen in the days of the Model T Ford, cranked by one of the pilots while the hose was held in place by the boom operator. Not exactly the picture of advanced aeronautical engineering. I cannot remember how many times I came home at night after a mission with oil all over my flight suit and shoes (another reason not to bother shining my shoes). The drum was "cleverly" placed next to the hatch that led to the lower deck. At the bottom of the ladder to the lower deck was what we called the APU or auxiliary power unit, a gasoline-fired generator used on the ground. It was easy to spill oil that ran down through the hatch unto the APU, which the next time it was started, could and has burst into flames.

I distinctly remember long overseas flights where the flight engineer told us we need to shut down an engine during the flight to make sure we had enough oil left so that we could use all four engines on landing, where we needed them for safety reasons.

The four propellers were prone to develop cracks due to vibration and/or metal fatigue and had been known to break up in flight, throwing pieces of propeller blades into the fuselage (like antiaircraft rounds). If they hit a tank, of which we had a lot, it was the end. So you can see that the role of a flight engineer was, among other important tasks, important for the continuation of flight by keeping those propellers in sync, and we had switches he constantly toggled to do just that.

The KC-97's upper and lower deck were both very roomy, and the fuselage had been widened to accomplish just that. I always thought it reminded me of a pregnant grasshopper, with its large green house glass front and slightly bulged out fuselage. The upper deck, as SAC configured it, was a row of tanks along one side of the cabin and bench seating along the other. The flight deck, entered from the upper deck was quite roomy I always thought with the pilots sitting just in front and below the flight engineer who was placed in a central position who could look out to the front and see what the pilots were doing or turn 90 degrees to a large panel filled with gages, detailed enough to give him good info on the engines and any other data he needed. He also could control RPM and had a series of toggle switches for syncing the props as I remember.

I sort of thought of his positioning as a "throne" from which he controlled his empire.

Behind him sat the navigator as his desk and across the cockpit was a chair for the boom operator to use on takeoff and during flight as he needed. Just behind the flight engineer's position on the floor was a trap door, located in the center of the rear portion of the flight deck. The door, or hatch if you will, led to a lower compartment directly below the flight deck that contained just about all our electronic gear: radio transmitters, radar, etc. It was commonly called the hellhole, due to the heat generated by the equipment and no ventilation. One could feel the warmth of the floor of the flight deck coming from the compartment below, hence hellhole. The hellhole was a potential source of electrical fires, and it did not disappoint. Directly over the hatch to the hellhole was a ceiling port for the navigator to take celestial navigation shots with his sextant, part of his regular trip routine.

At the rear of the aircraft, a portion of the fuselage below the horizontal stabilizer was replaced with a clear canopy over which was a platform for the boom operator to lie flat on his stomach, look down and out through the window in order to see the approaching bomber, communicate with the pilots thereon, and use his control stick to "fly" the boom into the bomber's intake port. One of the better contributions of Boeing to the Cold War was the development of the steerable telescoping boom for use in air refueling and was vital in the ability of SAC to develop the effective deterrence capability that it did. The boom had a ruddervator on the end that enabled the boom operator to fly it within a prescribed envelope, and it was telescoping so that it could be inserted in a bomber refueling port.

The B-47, as a sweptwing jet aircraft, needed a higher air speed to keep from stalling than did the KC-97. As gross weight increases, the minimum speed goes up, as it does for any aircraft. In order to keep the B-47 from stalling out as the on boarding fuel from the 97's tanks was pumped, both aircraft needed to increase speed. In most cases, the tanker was already running its engines and propellers at near maximums, so a gradual descent was required to help the tanker's speed gradually increase to match the bombers requirement to avoid a stall. (B-47s did at times stall and fall off the boom, some with really bad results.) The descent procedure was called tobogganing. As time passed and the B-52 became operational with its superior power, we did not need to descend during refueling since the B-52, if it needed more speed, just pushed us. I remember the feeling when a B-52 was hooked up. It was like, I would imagine, getting a "goose" in the rear.

Before we move on, there was another problem with the compatibility of the KC-97 with the bomber force. We used different fuel that flowed through the same plumbing system in the KC-97. The engineer had, at his station, a set of valve switches that controlled the flow of all fuel on board. There was a specific procedure to preclude the inadvertent mixing of the two. It was not a problem for the bomber, which could use both the aviation gas that we used and the JP-4 jet fuel they used. JP-4, if mixed with aviation fuel, would cause our engines to overheat quickly to the point of meltdown. Any mixing was carefully avoided, and if we were planning a long trip where we needed to use the JP-4 tanks for aviation gas, they had to be flushed out prior to filling them. As you would imagine, mistakes happened, and engines froze up.

C H A P T E R   7

Crew Duty

I was assigned to fly with a crew that needed a self-starter as a copilot. There was something missing in the crew's morale. Communications were not real positive. The flight engineer was a little cynical. The aircraft commander, a captain stuck in grade with close to twenty years in service, was not going anywhere and was going to retire as a captain. He was one of those disappointed airmen that served through two wars but were now not promotable and were in a career dead end. He could fly, but I am not sure he was interested in doing so anymore. Most of his time came in C-47s, the transport workhorse of the forties and fifties. His name was Ed.

The flight engineer was a tech sergeant with time in B-29s and B-50s prior to ending up here. (Seemed like that described the career path of a good deal of the squadron.) I never knew his first name, but I addressed him as Sergeant Mike. He was suspicious of young lieutenants from ROTC and like most flight engineers, prayed for capable pilots who might keep them alive. I can imagine what the nonpilot crew members were thinking when a new young pilot shows up to take their fate in his hands. The AC acted like he was over the hill, and here comes a young ROTC lieutenant, who, as far as they knew, would only add to their worries about going home at night. I liked him.

It took a while to for the flight engineer and boom operator to smile when they saw me show up at the plane, but eventually they did.

The navigator was young and new and like me, disappointed at ending up in a SAC tanker squadron as a navigator. He wanted to go to pilot training but had an eyesight problem, so he went to navigator school instead. He was over six feet, well built, and probably played sports in college. He like to drink and party and was not married. He was not happy with Ed. His name was Jerry.

I could see why I was assigned to this crew. Something was missing, and the operations officer needed to prop up the crew. A typical tanker squadron needed a minimum number of what was called a combat crew, in order to be declared combat ready by SAC Headquarters. For a squadron to be downgraded to noncombat-rated status due to a shortage of combat ready crews was a disaster for the squadron commander and probably for the wing commander.

Security clearances sometimes stood in the way of getting a crew combat ready. The clearance procedure and apparently the pilot increase needed for SAC created a problem. Clearances did not show up before the crew member was needed to become operational. At that time, if you were going fly in a USAF plane, you had to have, at least a secret clearance. To participate as a SAC crew member, you needed a top secret clearance. I remember many new crew members who were on the job before their top secret clearance arrived. However, one could not participate in the top secret commander briefing.

We were all happy to get our top secret clearances. It was a morale booster to know you had something "special."

Each wing had a war assignment as did the subordinate units in the wing. Our squadron had a specific mission in time of war, and during my stay in SAC, we were constantly being required to brief the wing commander as to our part in the scheme of things in the war plan. The briefing consisted of the wing (or in some cases the division) commander sitting alone in a briefing room while each crew member stood on a stage behind a podium and recited from memory their part in the assigned mission they might be asked to undertake in case of an enemy attack. We were graded on our pre-sentations, as was the squadron as a whole, and unsatisfactory pre-sentations had to be repeated and was a thorn in the career of the squadron commander.

As a eager young officer with some speaking experience (bingo night in Blythe), I had no trouble doing my part.

While in Little Rock, our main mission was in flying training missions with the B-47 pilots that the wing was training. That meant hours of flying level refueling platforms at altitude so that the bomber pilot trainees could practice the very tedious but critical hours practicing air refueling. The KC-97 was equipped with a weak autopilot that did not hold altitude well, so hours of hand flying were in order for the tanker pilots. This feature added to the complications of long distance/overseas trips.

I was good at holding a steady, level course, so I did a lot of the "platform flying" the mission required, and I was cool with Jerry and the flight engineer.

Everything had settled down, and we had settled in with our new life in Little Rock when the squadron was called in for a secret briefing. The squadron was going to go on temporary duty (TDY) to Lajes Field in the Portuguese Azores for about one hundred days. This was to be one of the last extended TDYs that SAC would be doing with tanker units since it was very hard on families and bad for retention.

Our mission there would be to support deployments and rede-ployments of B-47s to and from overseas alert positions in England, Spain, and Morocco by providing refueling over the Atlantic and standbys in the aforementioned countries for emergencies. We would be based in the Azores and rotate crews on two-week shifts to Spain, England, and Morocco and then back to Lajes Field, on the island of Terceira about one thousand miles directly west of Portugal and Spain in the Atlantic. It was an American base and about the same latitude as San Francisco, but I must say with much more unpleasant winters. Rain, fog, and damp weather seemed to be the norm in winter. I remember only a couple of sunny days while I was there.

The briefing officer announced that this was a secret deployment, and we were not to discuss this with anyone, not even our wives! Really! Try that sometime! Nevertheless, when I returned from this trip, I would be not only a seasoned pilot but a seasoned crew member.

When the time came for departure, the squadron of about twenty-two planes took off at intervals for Bermuda for a refueling stop and then Lajes. The KC-97s had plenty of room aboard, in addition to tanks for refueling, to carry troops and supplies, so we were a self-contained enterprise, so to speak. It was a long flight since it was across the mid-Atlantic, around the "fat" part of the globe as opposed to the fights to Europe across the northern part of the globe, called the great circle route, which cut hours off the route we were taking.

It was a tiring flight in a KC-97, due to the attention the crew had to pay to the operation of the large but complicated oil-eating engines and an autopilot that did not like to hold altitude. Since we all were transporting ground support personnel plus supplies, we had a load. Passengers walking back and forth in the main cabin, perhaps walking up the latrine and walking back to their seats, would cause the plane to change attitude enough to cause constant attention on the part of the pilots to keep the plane at a level altitude by constantly adjusting the altitude control on the autopilot. To mitigate this problem, ground support personnel being transported were not told there was coffee on board, were concentrated as much as possible in one area, and given blankets to keep warm. Then the cabin temperature was turned down with the plan that the passengers would huddle under the blankets, go to sleep, and not be walking around making work for the pilots. If they asked for coffee, we had none.

Really, not too different than the way paying passengers are treated by the airlines today.

Our trip was long and boring. The stop in Bermuda for refueling did not last near long enough. Finding a relatively small island in the Atlantic with the available navigation aids available in those days seemed tricky to me. We relied heavily on celestial navigation to determine the effect of winds. After hours of "boring holes," we got the island in site on radar and were only fifty miles off course. After landing, I found out that seven airplanes were laying over in Bermuda with engine changes. A comment on the complication of the R-4360 engine. I remember two good things about Lajes. One was that it had a SAC length runway (over ten thousand feet) and nice approaches on both ends. The runway was on a protrusion that allowed water approaches either way. I can never remember seeing the whole island at one time while flying over it. It was either night or bad weather. One day we were able to get a vehicle and do some driving around when the sun was out, and I was impressed with the number and grid of low rock walls that are used by the Portuguese to divide up family land after the death of a household head.

The other thing I have a pleasant memory about when it comes to Lajes was the Madeira wine that could be purchased there by the case at extremely low prices (maybe fifty cents a bottle) to bring back to Little Rock upon our return. It was not produced on that island, but in the Madeira islands some distance to the south but which were also under the control of Portugal and was brought up to Terceira by ships. It is a delicious sweet wine that we all drank at home back in Little Rock and took with us to restaurants where it was common to do so.

Since I never could sleep on the planes, I stayed awake and minded the plane while other crew members napped, except the flight engineer, who was always on the job. That made me a valuable crew member. Someone had to play with the autopilot and answer the phone (so to speak).

I still can't sleep on a plane, at least sober.

After landing and unloading everything and settling in our quarters, the CO called a briefing to go over how things were to be done at Lajes. Among them was a warning especially meant for the ground crews about frequenting brothels, of which there were several just off the base. Having located them on a map, presumably to let the troops know what to stay away from, he lectured on the dangers of VD known to occur at those places. He was still talking when I noticed enlisted personnel getting up and leaving.

"Why are they leaving?" I asked our flight engineer, a veteran of these trips.

"The CO just told them where to go to get in trouble. They did not know the locations of these places before."

CHAPTER 8

RAF Station Brize Norton

The crew had been participating in refueling operations for deploying B-47s for a couple of weeks when we were ordered to take two KC-97s to England and more specifically to RAF Station Brize Norton, northwest of London in what is called the Midlands area. The base had been taken over some years earlier by SAC and as SAC always did, lengthened the runways for multi-engine bombers and tankers. B-47s were currently stationed there as well as other bases in the Midlands, and a tanker detachment was deployed there in case a bomber coming from the US became short of fuel due to headwinds or was diverted to Spain or North Africa due to unexpected landing weather. We would keep a tanker on short alert and ready to launch on short notice with a backup tanker on a longer alert cycle. The crews would rotate from short alert to long alert to a day off. We were housed in a typically English two-story Tudor-looking facility with a bar and mess downstairs and quarters upstairs. The whole thing could have come out of a movie set.

We were scheduled to depart Lajes Field late at night. This was a typical SAC departure time, arranged they said so that we would land at dawn at our destination when unforeseen winds would be at a minimum. To say I was excited about going to England was an understatement. First, we were getting off the rock (Lajes) we were on, and second, as aspiring pilots, we had been subject to all the then books, stories, and films about Britain's RAF role and history in WWII. We were not that far away from those years. One of the books that we all read in our pilot training days was about Douglas Bader, the RAF pilot that lost his legs and therefore could take more g's than a two-legged pilot and was a hero. Not that anyone wanted to lose their legs, but we were going to an RAF station where pilots like him were based during the Battle of Britain.

On that flight, I made one of the few mistakes I made during my flying years.

We departed as planned, headed northeasterly toward Ireland, where we were, after crossing a radio beacon, to make a right turn heading east across southern Ireland, Wales, and then into the Oxford area and Brize Norton. We would expect dawn when we crossed the Irish Sea into Wales.

Easy.

After we leveled off and set our course, Ed and Jerry decided to nap. As usual, I would fly the plane through the night. Not a problem. I needed to be on the alert for the expected radio beacon signal so I could wake everyone up and start our inbound procedures. It must have been about three hours or so later that a female voice with a British accent boomed into my head set with our call sign. To say I was caught off guard would be an understatement.

"Wow, just like the movies," I shouted. Everybody, listen to this." I could visualize the controller with a headset standing over a large horizontal map and pushing a plane symbol with a long stick. She was issuing some instructions. I was not listening. But then I thought I picked up the radio beacon signal that would start our turn. I told her we were good (or something like that). I told Jerry we had crossed the beacon and was turning to 090, which was directly east, to start our Inbound leg to Brize Norton.

Everyone was up by then and ready for our eventual approach. It was still dark, and we were over a cloud layer and in and out of the clouds. Time elapsed.

We flew on. Dawn was breaking, and so was the cloud layer. All of a sudden, we were out of the clouds, and there in front of us was a large land area. "I did not know Ireland was this big." I was looking for the Irish Sea. No sea. Maybe we were already over Wales. I was waiting for a call from Midland control. Finally it came.

Midlands radar had picked up our IFF signal (an identification code). We were over southern France heading for the French Alps. I had turned early on the radio beacon, probably somewhere at the northwest tip of Spain.

"You need to make an immediate 180-degree turn," said the male voice. Not quite so friendly. Midlands approach had us and would guide us back across the English Channel and into Brize Norton. The British had really great radar capabilities.

Who to blame?

We wrote up the radar set. It had failed. Everyone knew they were faulty. The matter died. I kept quiet for a couple of days. We settled in at Brize Norton for our alert. It was quiet for a couple of days when Jerry got me. He had become close to the operations officer. He had that type of personality.

"We have a mission, Gene. SAC has authorized a weekend R & R [rest and rehabilitation] trip for the ground crews at Lajes to London. Morale had become bad since someone was arrested by the MPs going to a brothel and the base commander had grounded everyone," he said.

"So?"

"The squadron commander wants us to time the arrival of the plane here so that he can get the last train from Oxford to Cambridge and then he can visit on old friend for the weekend. Our job is to do the groundwork, working backward from the scheduled last train departure and the travel time from the base flight line to the rail station so as to arrive at the proper landing time."

So we got the jeep, drove into Oxford to the train station, got a train schedule, and then timed the trip back to the base and onto the flight line to the spot where the incoming KC-97 would be parked. Then Jerry calculated the flying time from Lajes using forecast winds, and the resultant information was called back to operations at Lajes so that the takeoff time could be called into SAC headquarters, who controlled all international flights.

The day of the arrival came, the plane was en route to England when suddenly, as seems to happen in England that time of the year, a pea soup fog developed. The plane was diverted to Lakenheath, a nearby base also used by SAC.

The fog was so thick that vehicles were grounded. When finally the fog lifted, the passengers arrived by bus from Lakenheath. It was too late for them to do anything, so Jerry and I decided (with some encouragement) to go into Oxford and round up some girls for a party at the base. With Jerry and his personality on hand, we did just that. Off we went. We convinced some girls in a local bar of the importance of their help in our common effort to protect the West against the threat of communism and returned with a jeep full of help. A good time was had by all, and Jerry and I got good marks.

The stint at Brize Norton and the concept of alert forces was really brand new to me at that point, but I was going to learn and experience much more severe alert situations and what it meant to our lives.

After our tour at Brize Norton, we were scheduled to repeat the same type of standby alert at Torrejon Air Base just outside of Madrid. The contrast as to the political make up of these countries could not be more severe. England, with its history of dedication to the rights of the individual and western culture, was a far cry from the world of Francisco Franco's Spain.

CHAPTER 9

Torrejon Air Base

The US (SAC) and Franco's dictatorship had one thing in common: halting the Soviet Union from taking over Western Europe. Franco was possibly more driven to it than the US. During WWII, Franco contributed troops to Hitler with the caveat that they only fought on the Russian front. That was only a little more than ten years before the US began construction of its needed improvements to the airfield that was the headquarters for the Spanish Air Force (such as it was). Housing, aircraft support facilities, and the longest runway in Europe at that time would be constructed to accommodate SAC bombers. The runway was thirteen thousand feet long. Any multi-engine pilot commanding an aircraft with a wartime fuel load had to be impressed. While KC-97s used fairly reasonably amounts of runway for takeoff with a big fuel load, I was to find out later that a KC-135 with a maximum fuel load would probably use 85 percent of that length on a day when the elements were not on the pilot's side. It reminds me of an old saying: "Two things you can't use in flying are altitude above you and runway behind you." In some cases, this runway mitigates on the latter.

The weather seemed to always be good as compared to the Midlands of England and approaches easy. The control tower at the field was operated by the Spanish Air Force, and like the rest of Spain at that time, they did not seem to know or use much English. It seemed like the tower controllers knew about ten words of English, "you are cleared" being the top 3.

SAC occupied the area on one side of the runway while the Spanish occupied the other. On the SAC side sat sleek-looking B-47s with their six jet engines slung under the wings, while on the Spanish side, the most noticeable parked aircraft were a couple of German tri-motor high-winged aircraft with an engine on each wing and one on the nose. It was like an early WWII or late WWI news reel in black and white. One day I remember watching from across the base as the Spanish practiced low-level parachuting from one of the trimotors. It was some sight.

Our detachment of KC-97s consisted of two crews and two aircraft. Like at Brize Norton, one crew was on twenty-four-hour standby and the other had twenty-four hours off. Notice I said *standby*, not *alert*. There is a big difference, since any launch would be staged on a step-by-step basis. The ranking officer of the detachment was the detachment commander and had a lot of authority over what we did on the ground. All flights were controlled by SAC headquarters in Omaha. They had a long arm. The detachment had the use of a four-door Ford sedan with Air Force dark blue vehicle color but no Air Force markings. It was used to drive from the base to the outskirts of Madrid, but driving in the heart of the city was discouraged due to the different culture-related to traffic rules, headlight use, and possible conflict with the Guardia Civil, who had lots of authority and carried machine guns.

On our first day off, we headed for Madrid. After parking in a recommended area on the edge of the edge of town, we decided to walk into the central area. Now I thought my education was going to be a good thing. I approached one of the many serenos (or watchmen) and in what I thought was good Spanish, asked the directions to a good restaurant since it was late afternoon and we had not eaten since breakfast. He smiled and indicated that we should follow him, which we did.

After about thirty to forty minutes of walking and having obviously reached the central district, we were ushered into a very formal-looking two-story building and led to the second floor. This was the Bank of Spain. There we were taken to a desk where a bank interpreter was seated. The serrano went over to talk to him and then he came over with a smile on his face.

"Good afternoon. The gentleman has brought you here because he did not understand anything you said, but because he thought you were Americans, he equated that with money and therefore you needed to come here."

Swell, I thought, *how am I going to break this to the crew that was tired and thirsty since it was a warm, dry day.*

I hedged, explaining to the crew that the interpreter knew of the best restaurants, and he did not know any. I am still not sure that worked, but I retreated from my position of informal tour leader. The problem was that I was taught Castilian, and they did not speak that in Madrid. Nevertheless, the banker recommended a good restaurant nearby that we would like, and it served good authentic Spanish food.

He was right. It was located in a walk-down part of a building lined with old brick and arches and served a great roast pig meal. I recently talked to a friend who had been in Madrid who had eaten at the same restaurant. Apparently it was the oldest restaurant in Spain and quite famous. After we had eaten, we took a cab to the Castellano Hilton. The base had reserved a large suite for use by some visiting dignitaries who did not stay as long as planned. The suite was still paid for, and we were encouraged to use it. It turned out to be their presidential suite, consisting of two well-appointed floors with large windows. I took away with me a small crystal ashtray that had the name of the hotel engraved on the bottom. I put it in our living room when I returned home and kept it there for a couple of years. Marge sort of looked at it with a less than enthusiastic look, and after a while it disappeared. (I was talking today with my neighbor and friend who served as a school teacher to children of American personnel at the base, and she remembered going to the Castellano Hilton on special occasions as it was the place to be in Madrid at that time. Small world.)

If we wished to visit a club, we were told to visit the "American bar." The cabdrivers knew where that was. It was an "all-American" atmosphere, full of personal from the base. There were military police dressed in nifty blue blazers and gray flannel slacks. No way would they look like MPs (or APs) except for a small metal name tag with a SAC insignia. Yes, that was the name of it—the American Bar.

I loved Madrid as is was then—little or no traffic, great-looking old buildings, friendly people (even though most could not speak English), and of course, the siesta, which shut everything down for two hours in the afternoon. Because of that, top restaurants and nightclubs did not open till 9:00 p.m. We did not attend any.

Madrid was a city with lots of police of different grades, from the Guardia Civil at the top to the sereno, or block watchman, at the bottom. No pickpockets, scammers, or street crime. About fifteen years later, after a democracy was established, Marge and I returned to Madrid for a visit, and all the above was present. It changed the nature of the city.

After a couple of weeks, we were ordered back to Lajes Field. When we were ready to depart, we got a notice from SAC that our flight would be delayed twenty-four hours due to weather conditions at Lajes. Okay, we can live with that. Jerry and I decided to visit the base officers' club, where drinks were cheap (around twenty-five cents), and we were looking forward to a pleasant evening. After a couple of hours and several drinks, someone located us to tell us that SAC had changed its orders. The weather at Lajes had cleared, and we were to depart within the hour.

Jerry and I were both suffering from too much cheap scotch. We could not tell Ed, who had stayed in his room listening to opera on his recorder, that we were not able to fly and report that to SAC headquarters in Omaha. So we tried to act sober and got on with it. Ed and I, like most crew pilots, traded off on every other takeoff and landing. It was Ed's turn, thank God. I could get away with my condition, I figured. However, when we lined up to take the runway, the tower cleared us to depart on runway.

"Thirty," I replied. "Left or right," meaning there were parallel runways and which one were we cleared on?

The tower replied, rather sharply, "Only one runway."

Ed gave me a funny look. I rubbed my eyes like there was something in them. He frowned. It was time to add power and go. Conversation over. Thank God.

Our flight path to Lajes was not direct as we were not allowed to overfly Portugal, which, as we all know, separates a large portion of Spain from the Atlantic and lies directly in the way of a direct flight path to Lajes. Overflight of countries by military aircraft can be diplomatic problem, even in peacetime. So we had to fly south to the Gibraltar area and then turn west in order to avoid Portugal. Jerry had retired to the cabin and gone to sleep on the passenger bench. I was in better condition and remembered the heading to Gibraltar, which was not hard to find, even in the night. The problem was we needed a heading for Lajes, some hours away to the west, a small target in a large ocean. I shook Jerry and woke him up. "We need a compass heading for Lajes."

Usually coming up with the right heading would consist of analyzing winds aloft, which seriously affect long flights over the Atlantic. Half awake and perturbed at being disturbed, he grunted at me, "West."

I went back to the flight deck and told Ed, who had settled into a conversation with the flight engineer, "Head 270," the compass demarcation for *west* and which sounded better than *west*. This was literally a shot in the dark.

I retired to the cabin and, in a departure from my normal habits, went to sleep, one of the rare times I slept on a plane. The booze helped. I woke up later and shook Jerry. He was starting to wake up also.

"What is our heading?" he asked.

"I will check." I walked up to the flight deck. Ed was in a conversation with the flight engineer. "Ed, what heading are we on?"

"West, of course."

I went back and told Jerry we were on the heading he gave us. That frightened him. He got up and went to his navigator station. Dawn was starting to break. We had no idea of where we were. I decided I had to break the news to Ed. As I turned to talk to Ed, I could see a beacon just coming into view at about the eleven o'clock position. It had to be Lajes. I pointed it out to Jerry, and he got on his radar. Sure enough, we had hit the island almost dead on after hours of flying over the Atlantic. Ed congratulated Jerry on his navigation. After we landed, Jerry looked into the weather we went through. We had flown through a low pressure area that had probably pushed us 150 miles north in the counterclockwise direction of the wind on the back side of the low and then brought us back on the front side, leaving us heading into the islands.

Sidi Slimane Air Base, Morocco

After a couple of weeks flying refueling missions out of Lajes, we were sent out again to do alert for deploying B-47s at Sidi Slimane Air Base in the northwestern part of Morocco. Sidi Slimane was one of three bases developed in that country in the early fifties by SAC for basing bombers pointed at the Soviet Union and close enough to reach it without refueling. The B-47s could make it from the bases we are talking about here. Morocco, which used to be French Morocco, was in the process of getting rid of France, but due to a treaty in existence, SAC was able to build the bases anyway. They would last a little over ten years before the US was asked to leave.

Located in northwest Morocco near the small city of the same name, Sidi Slimane was about an hour or so bus ride to the port city of Kenitra (at the time renamed from Port Lyautey, a French name selected when France had the power to do so).

As I remember, it was a dry, arid climate, and although there was green plants, one could see it was close to a desertlike atmosphere. At that time, there was not much there, although I understand it is now more "built up." My remembrance of the place was that of a French Foreign Legion post with a control tower and long runway. I sort of expected to see George Raft walking around (from the movie *Moroccan Outpost*). Someone wrote that "it was a dung heap with sand." I did not think it was that bad. But maybe that is because I was not there long enough.

Two things I remember about Sidi Slimane: one was an experience with a headset stolen from our aircraft, the other a trip into Kenitra.

In order to gain access to our KC-97, one, after gaining access to the base, had to be allowed on the flight line. That required a secret clearance and flight line badge. Once on the flight line, one had to pass through a checkpoint to get into the barbed wire that surrounded the SAC area. To do that, you needed to have the flight line badge and know the password of the day. Once inside the SAC area, where each aircraft had its own MP guard, one had to know the password plus be on the roster for access to that aircraft. One would think that the security was adequate.

When our aircraft was parked, pilots left their headsets with the boom mikes slung over the yoke. This is so it was immediately available in case of a required alert-type launch. Because the headsets were expensive and saleable, if you lost yours, you had to pay for the new one, which was several hundred dollars unless you got a report from the base provost that said it was stolen.

My set was missing one morning. I immediately went to the provost office to file a report in hopes of not paying for the new headset. I explained the situation to the provost, and he shrugged. "It was probably the Arabs. They are always getting into those planes." Really? Anyway, I got a new headset for free and was greatly relieved.

One of the other crew members and I decided to take a trip into Kenitra on our day off. As opposed to the situation in Spain, it was required to wear our uniforms. The only thing I could think of was to make sure the locals don't think we were French, which would not be good. We walked out the main gate and walked a short distance to the main road and bus stop. The bus was one of those you would expect to see in a typical African movie, complete with young men riding on the sides and on top of the bus. Inside there was nothing but men dressed in long robes with lots of embroidery and obviously room for weapons carried on the inside.

We found an empty seat and tried to make ourselves as little as possible. We were given strange looks but not bothered. No one smiled or said hello.

Kenitra seemed to be a sleepy town. Not too exciting, at least during the day. They were used to Americans there since there was a US naval air station just north of town. The biggest thing we did was to buy a camel saddle to take back to the US. They made good footstools and talking pieces. When we caught the bus back to the base, it was crowded with young people riding on the roof. The bus driver would not let us bring the saddles in the bus. He motioned that they had to go on top. I immediately felt this fear that that was the end of our camel saddles.

However, when we got to the crossroad that led to the base a few hundred yards down the road and the bus stopped to let us off, two of the young men on the roof handed us down our camel saddles (and smiled). So much for profiling.

A week later, we left for Lajes, and soon after, the squadron loaded everything up, and we all took off for our transatlantic flight home. The thing I remember about that trip was shutting down an engine for a great deal of the flight in order to save oil. The flight engineer was worried about our consumption of oil. Shutting down a second one was in the mix. Cruising on three engines at that weight was not a problem. With two, it was time to worry.

A couple of hours prior to crossing the American coast, we noticed an acrid smell drifting up from the compartment below the flight deck. The navigator was taking a celestial shot with his sextant, which was inserted into navigation port in the top of the flight deck and centered over the hatch that was the access to the hellhole. It is required when taking these shots that a period of time has to pass while the shot is in progress in order to get a valid one The navigator was busy with his shot and did not want to be bothered. Navigators never want to be bothered when they are taking a shot. His attention was focused on the sky and more or less refused to come down from the small table until his time ran out on his current shot. Meanwhile, the smell turned to smoke, and still the nav would not step down from his table. The smoke got worse. Finally I told the flight engineer to go ahead and pull the nav off the table and go down to the hellhole to see what was happening.

He jumped into action, pulling the complaining navigator down, opening the hatch and going down there with a fire extinguisher. He put out the small electrical fire, and we went on without any more trouble.

CHAPTER 11

Goose Bay

Marge was thrilled for me to be home. A hundred ten days is a long time, but the good news was that that was to be the last of the extended trips. Reflex, a program that had the B47s rotating from their overseas alert bases, was being extended to KCs. Now we would be gone for a little over 2 weeks, and we would do our war alert at Goose Bay, Labrador. The routine would be about 2.5 weeks at Goose and maybe a month home. During the home stays, we would do our training flights in support of aerial refueling training.

Goose Bay, a Canadian air base, was originally a fueling stopover for early commercial passenger planes traveling to Europe. Around the beginning of WWII, its use was greatly expanded for use by the Allied forces in transporting planes and troops. In the early fifties, SAC, as it did in many countries that added to its mission to provide nuclear deterrence, developed an operating base there in conjunction with the Canadian government. The USAF occupied one side of the main runway.

One of the uses was as a KC-97 alert facility, and 97s from several US SAC bases were sent there on a rotating basis to comprise an alert force of tankers prepared to refuel SAC bombers heading north in the event of war. The operation was part of the SAC "reflex" operations to rotate planes and crews in order to create more acceptability for aircrews and their families by cutting way down on the time away from home.

The KC-97, as I understood it, was originally designed to serve as a passenger and freight transport to serve the New York/Florida air routes. They definitely were not designed for the cold northern winters such as one experiences at Goose Bay. Our crews first trip to the Goose, as we came to call it, was in February, and it was memorable on several fronts.

The procedure was, as usual, to depart Little Rock at night, arriving at Goose Bay at dawn. This was done on a rotating basis with two to three crews and planes participating at a time. Upon arrival, we had the next twenty-four hours for crew rest before moving our KC to the "alert line," replacing a KC that would then depart for home. On Tuesday night, we could relax at the officers' club (or in the case of the flight engineer and boomer, the NCO club). Tuesday was half-price drink night, a break from the normal price of twenty-five cents.

As it turned out, the Canadian government itself had a significant presence at the Goose, where it had a regional administration center as well as other functions. In order to provide for the daily operations of the mission, Canada imported, on a one-year contract, lots of European and Australian workers, of which a large number were young single women.

That was a surprise. While the women were not allowed in the officers' club, a special club was established so that they would have a place to relax and enjoy themselves. That place was a rustic wooden building located on the flight line, where it probably was built as an operation and terminal for the early use of the airport for passenger travel. Now it was a western motif bar known as the Caribou Room, where good Canadian bourbon and Scotch could be purchased for a little as ten cents a drink. US wives, accompanying their officer husbands on duty at Goose, seemed not to be allowed in the club, but the Canadian women workers were.

More on this later.

There was a saying in SAC commenting on what might happen to an officer in an operational or support functions at a SAC facility, that if he screwed up, he could end up as snow removal officer at Goose Bay. The saying was based on the well-known problem that exists in keeping that base operational in the wintertime. While as far as I know, the Goose did not get as much snow as some of our western mountains do on an annual basis, it is a wet snow that severally injures the twenty-four-hour-a-day operation criteria required for an alert facility. It was widely believed by aircrews there that not only was the above saying true, but has happened. In addition, snowplow drivers were rumored to be enlisted airman that had the same fate.

During a snowstorm with low visibility, blowing snow, and long hours, snowplow drivers would run into airplanes and indeed, each other. For that reason, they were not allowed to plow within fifty feet on an aircraft (assuming they could make one out at that distance). So when they went down the taxiway in front of our plane, they left a bank of snow in front of the aircraft, just as snowplows leave a bank of snow at the edge of a road just plowed. This left the KCs cut off from the taxiway by perhaps a five-foot bank of snow. Since we were on fifteen-minute alert, the crews were called out to shovel the snow in order to make a pathway to the taxi way not only for the fuselage and landing gear, but four cleared areas were needed for the propellers.

I cannot remember when I had ever been as miserable as I was shoveling snow in the subfreezing cold dressed in arctic gear. Everyone got a shovel, and no one was excused from the activity. To add to the effects of subfreezing wet cold on the operation, our planes often developed cracks in fuel lines and other problems created by the cold. The airplane actually shrank about a foot, believe it or not. The control yokes in the flight deck, while in a locked position when we were parked, could be moved back and forth about six inches due to the air craft shrinkage. It was a standing order that due to the problem of oil congealing in the engine cylinders, aviation gas was pumped directly into the firing chamber to loosen up the congealed oil and the engines were started every other day. This caused spark plugs to be subject to fouling, and after so many starts, it was necessary to change spark plugs.

A KC-97 has four engines, each with twenty-eight cylinders, and each cylinder has two spark plugs. Do the math, as they say, and you can imagine what a task that was done in freezing conditions. Once we were woken up in the middle of the night and ordered into the briefing room for a special briefing. It seemed that a Danish ship with about seventy-five people on board had struck an iceberg near Greenland and was either sinking or had sunk. SAC headquarters had volunteered some KC-97s to do an impromptu search of the known location of the ship when it hit the berg. The idea being, I guess, that we had the fuel, were relatively close to the scene, and there was no one else.

The briefing was scary. The weather was blizzard conditions at the site of the search, high waves, bad visibility, and turbulence included. We were to fly about a hundred feet above the ocean looking for evidence of survivors. To my surprise, the briefing included several Danish reporters in coat and tie, there to cover the event.

Ed was not that sharp for this situation, and I did not feel I was capable of handling this huge, lumbering aircraft in these conditions, skimming over wave tops. On the way out of the briefing room, the flight engineer took me aside, knowing I was really worried, and confided, "Don't worry, Lieutenant, it will be fine."

When we got to the plane, it seemed that the ground crew reported a problem that would make us abort the mission. The nose wheel, which is needed for steering the plane on the ground and is controlled by hydraulic fluid, was inoperative. It seemed that the hydraulic line that supplied the steering control had ruptured in the cold weather, and there was a pink-looking sherbet material bubbling out of it. The flight engineer nudged me. "I told you not to worry"

I never will know for sure how that happened, but I knew we could not have made it back under those conditions. Out of the three crews, only one got airborne. That KC was commanded by the squadron's best pilot, whom we all admired. He made it back, reported that it was indeed bad, and they found nothing.

While these weather conditions were as bad as they were, summer and fall were quite nice there. In fact, near the base was a lake that had a fishing lodge used by General Le May for VIP summer fishing trips for important senators among others, who would be voting on the SAC budget needs. One of these was Brigadier General Barry Goldwater (RES), who was a big factor in the Air Force budget. Although I was not present at the time, the story goes that General Goldwater, arriving in uniform for his annual trip, went to the Caribou Room with friends the night they arrived for transport the next day to the fishing lodge. A very drunk Australian woman jumped in his lap and tore a star off of his shoulders with the comment, "I have never had a general before." Senator Goldwater was furious, I heard, and that was the beginning of the end for the Caribou Room, and it was shut down some time later. A couple of years later, when I was in the KC-135 program, we went into Goose Bay on a mission and I noticed that it was boarded up.

Marge was not one who liked to drink alcoholic beverages to any great extent (with a few notable exceptions), and it bothered her to hear and see the amounts of Scotch and whiskey that was brought home from overseas and the drinking it caused. I ignored it at first, but one Tuesday night at the Goose, having participated heavily in half-price drink night at the Caribou Room, I woke up the next morning laying on a bench made of cardboard boxes full of supplies. I had no idea where I was. I could see pine trees through a window, but that was it. I know of no pine trees on the Goose proper. I opened the store room door, and a lieutenant came over and asked me if I was okay.

"Where am I, and how did I get here?'

"You don't remember the party at the Caribou Room last night? You are at a radar site about ten miles from Goose. You insisted you wanted to see what a radar site looked like and rode home with us."

"I don't remember a thing." I looked at my watch, which showed that I had only about two hours till the briefing for aircrews, which preceded the replacement of a KC-97 with ours. I asked them how to get back, and they found someone who could drive me down the hill to the base.

I got back in time for briefing, but that was the end of any more serious drinking, even if the drinks were ten or fifteen cents.

CHAPTER 12

A Change in Direction

As I mentioned before, each combat crew member had a secondary job when not flying. Very often it was assigned to the crew as a whole and not just a crew member. Ed had been asked to work in operations doing scheduling of crew flying, an important function but not a popular one with crew members. Since everyone would fly about the same number of hours per month and make trips to the Goose in about the same ratio, the only thing left was: when? The scheduler of flying was subject to lots of requests for changes, and sometimes crew members got angry if they were refused. Using superior rank was not out of the question when the crew member outranked the person doing the scheduling.

After a week or so of doing this, Ed decided that fishing was better and called me to tell me to go into operations and replace him in his job for a few days while he went fishing. As my immediate superior, it was an order. So I went into the operations office and announced I was there to replace Ed. Although I was a first lieutenant by then, almost all the officer crew members outranked me.

It was a challenge to be sure, especially scheduling trips to the Goose, but I went to work with the resolve I could do this. It was not long before I was put in a brace (stiff attention while being yelled at) by a senior major who wanted to change his scheduled trip to the

Goose. I learned to say "yes, sir" a lot even though there was another answer (and the schedule remained as it was). Lots of excuses, lots of frustration. Scheduling trips on big holidays, wife's birthday, or wedding anniversaries were especially vexing.

I had a big board with an erasable surface that I learned to live with, taking it home at night to figure out how to make requested or necessary changes; calling up crew members and arranging crew substitutions was a specialty of mine. After a short time, the operations officer called Ed and told him not to come in anymore—I would be the scheduling officer. Not too long after that, I was told that I could no longer go to Goose when our crew was scheduled, since I was needed in Little Rock. So find a replacement. Ed was furious. He had been rejected, even though he asked for it, not I.

Working on scheduling called for ingenuity as well as humility. I was good at that, and I had complete backing by the operations officer and squadron CO. My duties expanded at the operation office, and I eventually became an assistant operations officer in some of the duties I was asked to perform, but crew scheduling was my thing, and the more I did it, the more I knew how to fix problems. I got to know everyone's special problems and how to fix it. Some of the reasons were strange. I got requests from crew members to get them on a trip to Goose because they had developed a relationship with a woman there and were, in fact, being summoned there by their girlfriend. One captain told me that he had to be there for his girlfriend's birthday, or she would write his wife. Being there for Xmas was a problem for a few who had demands at both ends.

Writing the wife was not a big threat, though, the way things were. Mail sent to squadron personnel went to the mail room at the squadron building, and wives were not allowed on the flight line. Safe haven as to say. I found out, however, that after I left the squadron, a new base commander at Little Rock AFB (responsible for all base logistics, including mail delivery), decided, without asking anyone, to get rid of the mail room clerks, eliminate the mail room and have all mail sent directly to the home.

The results were disastrous for morale. I understand ten families on the base got a divorce, and others suffered problems. Although this was unconfirmed, it had to have some truth. It was a surprise as to how much Goose-to-Little-Rock mail there was.

In addition to scheduling, I was assigned to give the weather briefing at premission briefings, which took place the afternoon the day before the mission. I would go down to the base operations office to meet with the base weatherman in the morning of the briefing, and he would give me a briefing and a weather chart for display at the mission briefing. I would then get up on the stage at the briefing and repeat, in my own words, what I had been told. I enjoyed that and tried to act like a TV weatherman and sometimes added my own touch to the briefing.

Meanwhile, Ed, who was still writing my annual officer effectiveness report (OER), a critical and important report that affected my promotion and assignment choices, told me because I was not going to the Goose anymore, he was going to recommend that I be grounded due to lack of interest in flying. To someone who was still thinking career, this was a blow and obviously done as retribution. I went to the squadron CO and told him this. "Don't worry," he said. OERs go through him for review, and he said he would take care of it.

Ed did what he threatened, and the CO called me in to show me an awful report and then he tore it up. "I want you to write your own report on yourself and bring it to me."

Okay, I could live with that. I was careful in writing the report so as not to look too good, but I certainly turned out to be a good officer and crew member. Ed never knew about the replaced report as far as I know, and I had no bad feelings toward Ed for what he did. He was part of what I had mentioned earlier, pushed aside by the system.

Shortly after that, the CO called me into his office and said that an assignment for a crew to upgrade to KC-135s (SAC's new jet-powered tanker) had come down from Fifteenth Air Force, and was I interested? "You can pick your own aircraft commander to take with you." I was not qualified for aircraft commander due to the requirement for more flying hours than I had. I told him yes. I would talk to my wife and John Purdy, who had become a close friend and was qualified due to his hours. John and I were looking forward to get an assignment upgrade to the KC-135. They were few and far between, and a KC-97 Squadron might expect only one or two per year at that time.

The assignment, after training, would be to Ellsworth AFB outside Rapid City, South Dakota, a definite movement north from the warmer climate of Little Rock, but that's where the base assignments for 135s were going. John agreed to go with me to the 135 program, and we soon left for Castle AFB at Merced, California, where the transition program for KC-97 crews was located.

Marge and I were off on a new and perhaps more serious assignment than we had seen. It would be good to get back to California, if only for a few months.

CHAPTER 13

The KC-135

To me, if I thought the KC-97 looked like a pregnant grasshopper, the KC-135 looked like a peregrine falcon. Outmoded now in the airline industry as a line carrier, it was developed to be the first jet passenger aircraft, partially helped in its development by Defense funding due to needing a tanker to match the new B-52. Out of that partnership came a safe and well-engineered airplane to serve the world as the first jetliner. Dwarfed today by its big brothers, the 747, the Dreamliner, and so forth, it was a significant achievement in the travel world. As for its refueling performance, compared to the KC-97, it was faster, could carry bigger fuel loads, and worked much better in the extreme cold of the northern bases, where it would be on alert. The air refueling tanks were isolated on a lower deck, leaving the main deck free for passenger carrying or cargo. And it was clean. No longer would I come home with an oil-stained flight suit. One could heat up a warm dinner in flight instead of eating cold box lunches. It was nice.

I have often wondered if the private sector need for a passenger jet, the Boeing 707, was what enabled SAC to get its much needed tanker, or the other way around, since the KC-135 was a 707 with modifications to make it fit the role of a SAC tanker. I believe it fit well except for being underpowered for the mission it was given. As I mention below, it created a problem to solve.

The problem with the danger of mixing JP-4 (jet fuel) with aviation gas was gone. We used the same fuel as the bombers. That had a downside, as I discovered during the Airborne Alert, but that is for later.

It was an aircraft that for the most part, was flown by a well-trained crew, and was able to accomplish the mission assigned. To me, the game was in the takeoff.

The KC-135 could carry almost twice the fuel load of the KC-97. Empty weight with crew was somewhere between 100,000 to 110,000 lb. After adding on a max fuel load, we would have a takeoff weight of just under 300,000 lb. I remember 297,000 lb. was the limit we could weigh, as that was what was calculated as the maximum weight we would taxi with and not collapse the landing gear. The SAC mission pushed the capability of the initial KC-135s, a situation that was later fixed when SAC replaced the original engines with fan-jets. But that was after my time. Fully loaded takeoffs, or "heavyweight takeoffs" as we called them, were a necessity to have the potential to carry out SAC's plans.

In order to support the need for more power for takeoff, SAC added a boost for takeoff by infusing into the jet engine compressors distilled water, which added density to the jet exhaust. The effect was that of an increase in jet engine thrust, which got us off the ground during heavyweight takeoffs. It was like a rocket-assisted takeoff and sounded about the same. About 900 gallons of distilled water could be injected into the engines by high-pressure water pumps, and it lasted about two minutes before water ran out. Hopefully when properly used, this would last through the takeoff, gear retraction, and flaps up and until we got climb speed. We used it a lot, and it was great when it worked right. The water was pumped into the engines by two high-powered British pumps, each pump serving one side of the plane. That was a problem.

The pumps generated a lot of heat when on and occasionally caused the circuit breaker to pop out, stopping the pumps' work. When a pump goes out during takeoff, not only do you lose the necessary push to get airborne, but suddenly you have a serious directional problem, what with one side getting water and the other not. The plane turned immediately toward the side where the pumps failed, pushing the plane off the runway if not corrected. There were two ways of correcting that: (1) reduce power on the other side, thereby resulting in a probable crash at the end of the runway or (2) forcing the circuit breaker to stay in (the circuit breakers were of the push-in, pop-out type), risking an electrical fire in the wing but ensuring a successful takeoff.

The second way was the only real choice. For that reason, the boom operator, whose takeoff position was seated in front of the large circuit breaker panel at the rear of the flight deck, was directed to keep a finger on each of the two pump breakers during takeoff. That way, not only could he tell if one popped, but he could push it in after receiving the command from the pilot doing the takeoff. It was extremely important for the pilot to give the command after the "boomer" announced the popping. Not that the pilots needed that information because the plane was already lurching to the port or starboard, but it was good to know that was the cause and not something else. This scenario lasted only a few seconds.

We were well trained in that procedure in the simulators, and when it happened, we know what to do. These 135s were known as "water wagons" because of that feature.

The navigator had a special job during takeoff. He sat in a jump seat between and slightly behind the pilots in order to see the airspeed indicator for the purpose of timing the aircraft acceleration during takeoff, a critical factor.

The takeoffs, were literally an "all hands on deck" event, especially the heavyweight takeoffs. All four crew members had an important role in the first minutes of flight. I located my old checklist, which I depended on for lots of things. One was computing takeoff information and writing it in with a grease pencil on a plastic-covered page of the checklist. It contained what we needed to know for a typical (in this case) heavyweight takeoff, for a given set of conditions. The data for that particular take off could still be seen on the page.

For the takeoff I had prepared for, the aircraft takeoff weight was 290,000 lb. We were probably carrying about 180,000 lb. of JP-4. (about 28,000 gallons). Once we were on the runway and cleared for takeoff, the pilot making the takeoff advanced the throttle to the preplanned EPR (exhaust pressure ratio, which was the primary indicator of power settings), the brakes were released. I hit the water turn on switch to start the water injection.

At 70 knots on the airspeed indicator, I said, "*Now*" to the navigator. He would start his stopwatch. Eighteen seconds had been planned to accelerate to 130 knots in this case. The navigator called out eighteen seconds. If we were at 130 knots on the airspeed indicator, we were good. If we had not made it, then an immediate abort was in order.

We had accelerated to 130 knots in the eighteen seconds (we usually did), so we continued.

The next charted speed was 141 knots on the air speed indicator. That was refusal speed. After that, we would be committed to continue the takeoff since there was not enough runway left to stop.

Takeoff speed had been charted at 171 knots on the airspeed indicator. We would use about ten thousand feet of a roughly twelve-thousand-foot-long runway at that point before the plane was rotated (which means bring the nose up to the liftoff attitude). At that point, we could no longer see the runway ahead due to the "nose up" attitude of the plane. We could see the ground out the side windows and feel the aircraft lift off.

There was no more runway left.

The landing gear was retracted and then the flaps brought up. About one thousand feet above the runway, we leveled off and waited for water to run out. Hopefully we were at or near climb speed.

Once we got to climb speed, the hard part of the flight was over. Time to relax. Less than three minutes had elapsed since we started our takeoff run. The rest of the flight could be expected to be smooth.

The above was repeated as part of normal operations on an ongoing basis.

One other feature of the KC-135 was a potential safety problem was the horizontal stabilizer. With a propeller-driven plane, the elevator, located on the rear of the horizontal stabilizer, was used to effect changes in the pitch of the plane so that the nose would go up or down. This, with either a power addition or power reduction, caused the airplane to gain altitude or descend. On a sweptwing multi-engine jet that is not enough surface to cause the necessary change in pitch. Therefore, the entire stabilizer moves, electrically operated. Due to the design, perhaps the only possible design, this is what was built. The KC-135 manual warned of possible "stabilizer runaway," and a cutoff switch was placed on the panel next to a large "trim wheel" set next to the aircraft commander's right leg in order to disable the power to the stabilizer, if a runaway occurred. The pilots were to grab the wheel to stop it if possible, while hitting the cutoff switch. Also putting the pilot's knee up against the wheel to help stop it, Because of this possibility, we wore light gloves most of the time. We were well trained in the simulator for this possible occurrence, and as far as I could remember, it never happened on any flight I was on.

CHAPTER 14

Castle Air Force Base

astle AFB, for years the home of SAC's Ninety-Third Heavy Bombardment Wing, which was the home of such aircraft as the B-36, was just outside Atwater, California, a short distance north of Merced, a major central valley town in California. It was converted to training KC-135 and B-52 crews in the late fifties. We found a duplex in nearby Atwater to move into, and I found a group to carpool with to the base. That made it comfortable now for Marge. Work hours were regular, and it was pleasant to be back in Northern California. We had had our second child, a girl, Marissa, by then, so it was easier for Marge to take care of them.

Transitioning to a multi-engine jet from a multi-engine propeller-driven plane was not that hard. We already knew multi-engine procedures as well as SAC and refueling tactics. There were, of course some significant differences in the power source and aircraft aerodynamics,.

The engines did not produce immediate power response as did the conventional piston engines powering a propeller. There was a comparative delay as the throttle was advanced and the plane responded. That was handled by thinking ahead a little more and understanding what to expect. The major power instrument to look at was no longer the rpm indicator but the EPR indicator—EPR meaning "engine pressure ratio."

The swept-back wings, while enabling the kind of performance needed in this type of jet, changed the dynamic stability of the aircraft as compared to a straight-wing aircraft. It was less forgiving than the straight wing.

Ground speeds were faster and decisions made faster. You had to stay one hundred miles ahead of the aircraft it seemed to me—seventy-five miles for sure.

But instead of being a "truck driver," handling an aircraft that required heavy handling of the controls, the 135 was handled best in a much more subtler and smoother way. One had to be lighter on the controls, the horizontal stabilizer, which controlled pitch, was controlled by an electrical thumb switch on the yoke. I liked it. This model of 135 we flew suffered, due to design features, what is called Dutch roll on final approach to a landing. The best way, at that time, to correct it was what is called cross control—short, sort of choppy movements with the yoke and rudder moving in an uncoordinated manner. That was not what smooth and coordinated pilots were used to, but that was a specialty of mine. I was chastised often in the past for a less than coordinated turn technique; this was what the doctor ordered for Dutch roll. It was almost automatic for me.

I was graded up for my landing techniques and ability to handle Dutch roll. John was a very smooth pilot who flew instruments with the best, but did not handle Dutch roll well on final approach. Coordinated use of the controls was an impediment to countering Dutch roll. In the future, when we flew together, I made a good share of the landings, and he handled instrument weather conditions when they were bad.

We made a good team.

It was 1960, a presidential election year. John Kennedy was running against Richard Nixon. Nixon, previously being Eisenhower's VP, had to continue Eisenhower's apparent policy of control of the Defense budget, set forth in his famous farewell speech, where he warned of the "military-industrial complex" and what it meant in terms of large budget expenditures on equipment. From what I could see, this was the same policy that had embittered many of the older serving officers who felt they were being left behind by Eisenhower and that feeling was easy for me to pick up on.

Kennedy, on the other hand, was for a strong military and a "manifest destiny" and for the US to be stronger in the world's eye. (Sound familiar?) Like my peers, I was for that. This was our first presidential election, and Marge and I went across the street where a woman had set up a voter registration in her garage.

I knew the way I was going—Democratic; a bigger, stronger military; bigger and better airplanes; more chance for promotion. After all, I thought I was a career officer at that point. Marge not so much.

In an interesting comment on changing times, when we went to register, the lady asked me what party. "Democrat," I said. Then she turned to Marge.

"And you?"

"Independent," she said.

"Is that all right with you?" the woman said, turning to me.

"No, make her a Democrat," I said.

"Okay," the woman said and wrote that down. Marge was livid, but kept it to herself till we got outside. I explained that it was for our future. She forgot about it several months later. (After we left the service, Marge became very active in the Democrat party, becoming chairperson of our local Democratic Central Committee and running the office of our Democratic congressman for several years.) I knew what was best for her.

I drove around the base with a Kennedy bumper sticker on my rear bumper for a while until I was stopped at the main gate one day and told I could not drive on the base with the sticker on my car while I was in uniform.

Soon we graduated from the training program, and Marge and I and the kids were on our way to Rapid City South Dakota, assigned to the Twenty-Eighth Air Refueling Squadron at Ellsworth Air Force Base. We had been at Castle for about six months.

All my training and experience as a pilot, as well as all the chips I could put on my shoulder, would become necessary at more time of the other during my assignment with the Twenty-Eighth.

CHAPTER 15

Ellsworth AFB

Ellsworth AFB, located about ten miles east of Rapid City, South Dakota, like so many US bases, evolved from a WWII Army air field and had become a major Air Force base with a bombardment wing, missile facility, and nuclear weapons storage, among other things. The KC-135 squadron there was part of the Twenty-Eighth Bomb Wing, with a full complement of B-52s at that time. To my dismay, while looking at a history of the base on Wikipedia, I saw no mention of the B-52s or KC-135 operations there during the late fifties and early sixties and the contribution that those units made to the success of the Airborne Alert operation that was important to the nation during our Cold War faceoff with the Soviet Union.

Rapid City, at the eastern foot of the Black Hills, was not the ideal location for a family that was used to California living, but it had its own thing. Summertime in the Black Hills was magical and the nearby old western towns of Deadwood and Spearfish created a tourist charm. Just outside Deadwood, there was a ski area where Marge and I eventually learned to ski. We were able to get base housing fairly quickly, and although it was not as good as Little Rock, it was suitable and close to the flight line. The base had a grade school for the children of those stationed there, and that helped.

The weather, especially the winter weather, had a few surprises. Being at the eastern base of the Black Hills, winter storms coming from the west brought windy conditions, as you might expect, that flowed down the eastern slopes of the Black Hills in an uneven pattern and spread over the Rapid City area, creating temperature increases that were not always felt evenly in the area. For instance, I remember being in downtown Rapid City in January, where you could find a forty-degree difference in temperature depending what street you were on. These winds are called Chinooks. Because of this, the area was called a banana belt. All in all, I would say, Rapid City was not a bad assignment as far as a place to live. The Black Hills were beautiful in the summer; the winter provided some skiing above Deadwood at a place called Terry Peak ski area, and we had good neighbors on base that we could count on to help each other when the husband was gone. Our neighbor across the street was a graduate of the University of Montana and a good skier. He taught Marge and I enough about skiing so we could all go up to Terry Peak for a day of winter fun, then stopping off at the Deadwood Saloon for hot buttered rum.

As to the Chinooks, while this was not such a big deal, but rather an oddity to the residents of the city, the changing weather conditions sometimes presented problems to SAC aircraft taking off at nearby Ellsworth since wind conditions could and would change at various places on the two-mile-plus runway at the base. The winds were at an angle to the northwesterly facing runway, creating more of a crosswind at times than was comfortable or safe for heavy tankers taking off. I remember going down the runway at Ellsworth, which, like most runways, had wind socks at both ends of the runway so pilots could detect crosswinds. I have seen the windsocks pointed in different directions from each other and indicating more than a breeze.

The Twenty-Eighth Air Refueling Squadron had recently been equipped with new KC-135s, and morale was good. We had two missions. One was to have crews and planes on alert for immediate takeoff 24-7. This was accomplished with an alert facility off the end of the runway, which was the usual direction of takeoff given historical wind patterns. Our crews spent a rotating twenty-four-hour duty confined to the facility along with the bomber crews we would refuel in the air in the event of a war. The alert facility was half underground, was new, and was well equipped for crew living. When the Klaxon sounded, signaling, almost all the time, a practice alert, we would dash out to the planes and report to the command post that we were ready to go. There was one time it was not practice.

Unlike the KC-97, which due to its limited speed as compared to the bomber it refueled, had to be geographically positioned in the far north to get a head start on the bomber, the KC-135 could take off and fly with the bomber it was going to refuel to the refueling point.

On one October night, I remember the Klaxon blaring, and when we got to the plane, the command post said this was not practice and to start engines. Starting engines was a big deal because everyone used fuel that was planned for the mission. If we did not go, all the planes had to be topped off in order to be ready to accomplish the planned mission if the whistle blew.

As to my memory, we taxied to the end of the runway before the alert was called off. Had we gone far enough to have retracted our landing gear, I would say we were at war.

As I mentioned earlier, there was a series of radar early warning radar lines in Canada, the Dew Line, the Pinetree Line, and the Mid-Canada Line. In the event communications was lost with these radar "fences," it was assumed that they had been taken out, a signal for attack.

That was what happened. The communications from all three lines was lost to NORAD. As it turned out and was quickly discovered, the land communications system for these radar sites all converged in one place before traveling to the US, and there was some kind of electrical problem at that point.

An electrical problem shut the station down and NORAD and SAC, as planned, started the planes moving. The outage was diagnosed before we launched, and we taxied back.

That was close. They fixed that problem I understand. I later read about the incident in a news source.

The other mission of our tanker squadron was to keep a keep a couple of tankers in Alaska to support Operation Chrome Dome, the SAC airborne alert. This task force of tankers gathered at Eielson Air Force Base, just outside Fairbanks, Alaska, where we joined tankers and crews from other outfits to form a task force.

John and I were able to stick together after we arrived, and our new navigator and boom operator fit in nicely.

CHAPTER 16

Eielson Air Force Base

The northerly location of Eielson, just outside Fairbanks in eastern central Alaska, made it a facility that has lots of strategic military uses. If one looks at the history of the units using the base they included a long list of tactical aircraft, including the old P-38 to the F-35 and B-29, among others. What I did not notice was the use of the base by SAC to support the Airborne Alert that I believe was the final blow to the Soviet Union in their quest to dominate the west. To have B-52s, carrying nuclear weapons, with the ability to deliver them, in the air twenty-four hours a day around your border has to be a huge headache. The crews that flew the B-52s on these long missions have, in my mind, not gotten the public acclamation they deserved.

However, in order to make it happen, they needed to be refueled in the north country in order to make the difficult trip from the US mainland up past Greenland and through the Arctic Circle and back to the US. That was the job of the 135s like those in the task force that was assembled at Eielson. The tour there was roughly two weeks at a time for each crew and plane, and lots of days we flew two missions a day.

We would take off, using just about the whole runway since we were loaded to the gills, as they say, not able to carry anymore.

I have described a typical heavyweight takeoff earlier carrying what amounted to the amount of JP-4 that would fill a modern full-size railroad tank car.

SAC had asked and was given a special appropriation hire contractors to cut down about a quarter mile of trees as the end of the prevailing runway after they discovered tree branches in the wheel wells of the first 135s participating in the mission.

After a scary takeoff (we used to joke that we could tell how much runway was left by the width of the navigator's eyes), we would climb on course to the north while the navigator would be contacting the scheduled B-52 to start a procedure to meet at the planned point. We would reach altitude, level off, and turn back toward the base to establish our refueling track. The bomber would come in, hook up, and refueling would begin. We would finish our refueling just about over the base (at cruise altitude) and start an immediate descent toward the runway we were going to land on. We had just enough fuel left to make a safe landing and taxi to the refueling area to get reloaded. That after taking off thirty to forty minutes earlier with enough JP-4 to fill a railroad tank car!

Then after refueling and a short break, we would start engines and do it all over again,

Occasionally we would have mission to go meet a bomber in the north Atlantic, which required a flight eastward from Fairbanks across the Arctic circle. I thought these were fascinating trips, crossing from day to night and then going back to day again on the return trip. These trips were also memorable due to what seemed long periods of radio silence, no other air traffic to worry about, and the occasional glimpses of the Arctic terrain through the clouds.

Since UHF, the normal band used for air-to-ground communications, was not usable, there was little calls to make. It seemed peaceful.

It was one of those flights that we got a call from seemingly nowhere with a strong American voice requesting our home base. It came over a UHF (ultrahigh frequency) radio channel. It was coming from a Russian fishing trawler cruising in Baffin Bay. We had been warned about this, so I was ready for it. UHF is basically "line of sight," so what ground station with American personnel would be operating there? The proper response was not to respond. If I did even challenge them, they would have learned two things—that we were an American plane and they were on the right frequency. Another time we gave too much fuel to a bomber. Bomber pilots were always asking for more JP-4 than they were scheduled for. They wanted to make sure they could get home for dinner and not land short at a strange base.

One day we made a mistake and gave them too much JP-4.

That left us short of fuel and not knowing at the time that a snowstorm was occurring back at Eielson. It had developed sooner than expected, with snow coming from the south and being rather heavy. The prevailing runway at Eielson was northwesterly in direction. That was the runway that had a precision approach, being an ILS (instrument landing system). That system had a radio wave that provided directional guidance and one that provided a glide slope so that if were on both paths, you could fly an approach to the runway in such a way as to execute a safe landing in very poor visibility conditions. The pilot's instrument panel has a display with a vertical line and a horizontal line that show where the plane is. If the two signals crossed in the center of the display, that meant you were on glide path and on course.

On the opposite end of the runway, there was a directional guide but no glide slope. Since the runway pointed to the south and into the wind, that was the runway we would have to land on, and as I mentioned, with no glide slope to tell us when we were descending on the right path to land in the first one-third of the runway for a safe landing. This was called a back course approach and not really acceptable for the weather conditions and low ceiling that existed.

We were notified of the landing choice on the way back from Baffin Bay. Our fuel situation was such that we had enough fuel for one approach and maybe a go-around. The ceiling was about five hundred feet. The only other alternate landing field was Yellowknife in the Canadian Northwest Territories. Too far. We had no other choice but to do a back course approach without a glide path.

However, we had a directional guide, and the navigator had an airborne radar and a radio altimeter that gave us our height above the ground. I got up from my seat and went back to his station with an approach plate that showed the layout of the back course. We figured out what the radio altimeter should be showing at selected distance from the runway, and he would call out the altitudes. I figured out a likely rate of descent (we had what is called a vertical velocity indicator at each pilot's station as do all airplanes so that the pilots could tell what rate they were climbing or descending) and a beacon on the ground that would tell us when to start the descent to the runway.

When we crossed the beacon, the navigator gave out the altitudes that we needed as we descended on the imaginary glide path.

All we could see was blowing snow out in front. We kept going. All of a sudden, I could see runway lights through the snow. We were high. We dropped full flaps and brought the throttles all the way back to increase our descent. By then we were below the ceiling and could see the whole runway. We touched down hard and fast. I hit the spoiler lever. Spoilers are panels that raise up from the top of the wing and add resistance. John worked the brakes. We stopped just at the end of the runway.

Would not want to do that again. By comparison, heavy weight takeoffs did not seem so bad.

CHAPTER 17

A Crew Change

Back at Ellsworth, our routine was a stable one. I was by then a captain and had been offered a regular commission to replace the Reserve commission that is given to an ROTC graduate. That meant I could stay for a career without fear of being released. I was career minded then, and Marge was good with her role. Then I was called in to the squadron commanders' office and told they wanted me to fly with an older major that they thought I could help out.

Major Tim, as it turned out, was a pilot with a long and distinguished career in the Air Force, having flown the famous Berlin Airlift in a C-47 amid terrible conditions. The Berlin Airlift occurred right after WWII, at a time when the Soviet Union was trying to control Berlin by not allowing US ground transport to travel to Berlin through their part of the Germany that had been divided up by the Allies. Even though Berlin was in the Soviet Zone, the US was in charge of West Berlin, provided they could get there.

The airlift was a challenge to Stalin, who, in 1945, wanted to freeze the US and England out of controlling any part of Berlin, which he had planned on dominating. The airlift was comprised of US and British planes ferrying food and other essentials into West Berlin through a narrow air corridor twenty-four hours a day. There was always a plane taking off or landing in Berlin and over three hundred thousand flights in all, I understand. Can you imagine the historical difference if the West did not have presence in the capital of Germany after WWII?

Due to the hours, weather, and other pressures, there were incidents. The major was a victim of that situation. The participants in the airlift were considered heroes.

He was very popular in the squadron, and he wanted to stay on flight status, and I would have to think that he was needed to be on flight status by the squadron. The squadron needed crew members. The major, however, due to aircraft accidents he had been in during the Berlin Airlift, was left with head injuries that could interfere with his ability to command an aircraft, let alone a four-engine jet.

Having said that, I should say he was a good and smooth pilot, and our relationship went well. Then one night we were returning to the base from a night mission and instructed to make what a penetration approach to the landing runway. A penetration is a military approach that begins when the plane flies over the runway at say twenty thousand feet and turns to a heading that is almost the reverse of the runway heading inbound for a landing. The idea was to lose about half of the altitude above the runway outbound, make a turn to the left or right, rolling out on the runway, heading and leveling off just before you crossed the outer marker, a beacon that signaled the start of final approach. The rate of descent during the outbound leg could be as much as four thousand feet a minute in order to descend without going out too far.

It was a moonless, clear night, and our outbound leg took us in the direction of the Black Hills, which were not visible in the darkness. We started around twenty thousand as I remember, descending outbound around four thousand feet a minute on the indicator. It was Major Tim's descent and landing (we would take turns). I kept an eye on the rate of descent as I talked to the tower about landing clearance. Suddenly I noticed the rate of descent increased when it should have been decreasing. I looked over at the major. He was slumped forward in his seat, and we were looking at a six-thousand-feet-a-minute descent on the indicator.

I grabbed the yoke and started bringing it back to stop the descent. I could not see the terrain, but we all knew there were hills out there. The boom operator saw what was happening and jumped out of his cockpit seat and helped bring the major back to a normal sitting position. I leveled the aircraft out, completed the turn into the runway, and was ready to go ahead and land.

Then the major woke up, took the yoke back, and went on the make the landing. After we parked and disembarked from the plane, he took me aside to chastise me for interfering with his control of the plane.

"Captain, if you ever try to do that again, I am going to write you up for insubordination."

"Yes, sir."

After he left, the navigator and the boomer thanked me for my action. I was not mad at him. He had no idea of what had happened. I kept my mouth shut out of respect and hoped that was a onetime incident.

It wasn't.

A couple of weeks later, we were scheduled for a heavy weight takeoff. It was the major's takeoff and landing turn. As I have mentioned, on a heavyweight takeoff, the boomer keeps two fingers on the pop-out circuit breakers that control the water pumps so that he knows immediately if one pops out. As we were approaching refusal speed, the plane started to lurch to the right.

"The starboard circuit breaker is out, sir," said the boomer into the intercom. The response from the pilot doing the takeoff should have been push it in.

No response. The plane continued to move to the right side of the runway. The boomer said it again, "Circuit breaker out." No response from the major. So I gave the order. "Push it in." He did. The plane straightened out, and we took off safely.

After we landed, the major took me aside. "I warned you, if you were insubordinate again, I was going to write you up, and I have had it." The navigator and boomer were listening. They headed into the squadron building for the operations office. They told the operations officer what happened and let me know they did.

I was told that the major did write me up on an effectiveness report, suggesting I meet a Flying Evaluation Board. His report would be normally submitted to the wing commander to go into my personal record. A few days later, the squadron commander called me in to tell me that he got the report and rewrote it for submission to the wing commander. He put me down as EWQ (exceptionally well qualified). A rating reserved for the top 10 percent of the officer corps as I remember. I do not think Major Tim ever knew. The crew asked me to stay, but of course, I could not.

I don't remember what happened to the major. I was not angry with him but sorry for him. He had contributed a huge amount to both the Air Force and the nation and deserved better than the situation he was put in.

I went back on John's crew.

One has to accept that in a military organization, just as in a private corporation, human relationship factors develop and sometimes corrupt or alter the basic rules the group is ruled by. In short, people are people, and favoritism, poor judgment, and mistakes often occur in the administering the rules when you are dealing with people you have come to know in the organization. Major Tim's case would be a good example of this. While it is not hard to see why he ended up in a seat he should not have been in, I am reminded of a somewhat similar situation that happened about the time of the incident discussed above.

Only this situation, while it only went so far, was just a matter of bad judgment. Period.

Captain Anderson, an older pilot who had been serving as a copilot for many years and accumulating many hours, was at the point he needed to upgrade if he was to stay on flying status. He failed his "check ride" required to make aircraft commander.

The operations officer took him off flight duty, and he was assigned to the squadron command post staff, where order and instructions are given to crews in flight. How would he do in that important position?

CHAPTER 18

Fun in the Sun

Because our crew, I would like to think, performed so well on assigned flights, we were asked along with another crew to do a ten-day mission out of Hickam Air Force Base in Honolulu to refuel a squadron of B-47s being returned to the US from the far eastern Pacific, the redeployment being staged over a week. This was not a bad assignment given it was February and weather around Rapid City was pretty cold. Our KC-135 was outfitted with airline-type passenger seats so we could take a contingent of doctors, dentists, and other medical personnel on an R and R at the same time. They would fly over to Honolulu with us and return with us when we were done with our mission.

Hickam Air Force Base, located just easterly of Honolulu, shares its runways with Honolulu International and has a civilian (FAA) control tower. We were instructed to contact the SAC detachment commander there when we landed, and he would instruct us on what to do as to our operations, quarters, etc., while we were there. However, when we landed, taxied over to the SAC area, and disembarked from the aircraft, the local commander was nowhere around. So we asked some of the personnel there and finally found someone to help.

"The colonel spends a lot of time at the beach. However, he checks in from a phone booth every hour, and we can tell him you are here."

That is definitely not the SAC we knew.

Eventually he did show up, and we got organized. The next morning, we did our first of several missions. They were close to heavyweight missions, but because we were taking off at sea level, there was a lot of mitigation since we could generate more power for takeoff. We took off one minute apart using water injection. The Waikiki hotel area was on the post takeoff path, so that created a lot of uncomfortable noise for the hotel guests at Waikiki. Without noise suppressors and at the low altitude at which we flew over Waikiki, it had to be bad.

Sure enough, after we returned, we were called into the colonel's office. "We have had a complaint from the Honolulu Chamber of Commerce that you are creating a noise problem with the hotel guests on Waikiki. We would like you to turn out to sea right after takeoff, turning inside the Aloha Tower." The Aloha Tower is a Honolulu landmark on the ship channel between the downtown area and the airport, and I guess was the first thing ship passengers saw when that was the way to travel to Hawaii and entering the harbor.

"Okay," we said, even though this was a rather dangerous turn to make at a low altitude and speed. The FAA tower chief had asked to fly with one of us to closely assess what was happening. I guess the hotel owners were really raising hell.

So we took off like the day before, only this time, after the gear was up, we made a thirty-degree bank to the right so to turn inside the tower. You could feel the stall buffeting that occurs before a stall, and we rode it right around the turn. The tower chief was looking a bit shaken but said nothing. After our return, we were again asked to meet.

This time, the University of Hawaii called. It seems they had a shark farm in the channel next to the Aloha Tower, and the sharks were going crazy with the vibrations from our water-enhanced exhaust. That settled it. We had to choose between doing good for the sharks or the tourists. Easy answer, the next morning we went right down Waikiki. It was a lot safer.

CHAPTER 19

The Seeds of Doubt

By this time, I was committed to what looked like a career in which I could do well. My family would have security while living within a community that offered support. Our mission was a proud one, and I was focused on what we were doing. Our world was bounded by the SAC mission, the people we lived among, and what we did every day. In some ways, Marge and I lived in a sort of island in the sea of a military world. The civilian world was far away.

From the backyard of my home at Ellsworth, you see the planes taking off when the southern-facing runway was used. The planes, especially the B-52s, would level off after retracting the gear and raising flaps in order to gain climb speed. There was a ridge a mile or so south of the runway. The B-52s would level off and then disappear over the ridge before starting a climb. Mark, my son, who went to elementary school at the base (first grade, I think) was standing with me watching a bomber disappear over the ridge, and he turned to me and said, "That's where Russia is." I asked where he heard that, and he replied, "The kids in school say that because that's where the bombers go."

I always remembered that.

One day we were scheduled for a Higher Headquarters mission. That meant a heavyweight takeoff for sure, and the mission would be controlled by SAC headquarters communicating through the squadron command post. It was a forecast to be a windy day, with westerly winds coming off the Black Hills that created a potential problem, especially with a crosswind with gusts that exceeded the safety envelope for a heavily loaded plane. The performance manual requires a higher takeoff speed if the crosswind component exceeded limits. It was hard to increase takeoff speed by holding the plane on the ground when our take-off roll was already predicted to take most of the runway length available.

Nevertheless when we started engines, the command post said conditions were acceptable and the mission was on.

We started down the runway. About refusal speed, we could feel the crosswind trying to pick up, pushing us to starboard, but more seriously, raising the port wing and thereby lowering the starboard wing. The direction of the wind and the sweep of the wing combined to give the upwind wing way too much lift as compared to the other wing. The port wing rose, resisting our joint attempts to hold the wing level and keep the plane on course with heavy rudder pressure. (Today 135s have power rudders that give the pilots better directional control, but not then.)

As we fought to keep control, I could see the outer engine pod on the starboard getting closer to the runway as the port wing kept wanting to rise. It was looking scary. Then the wind let up. The port wing came down. We straightened out and continued our successful takeoff.

As usual, after cleaning up the plane and arriving at climb speed, I contacted Denver Center for climb clearance. (Even military flights need ATC clearances when mixing with commercial traffic.) The traffic controller was surprised to hear from me. "Your flight was cancelled by SAC due to the dangerous crosswinds."

We went on and dumped our fuel in order to get down to landing weight and went home. After shutting the plane down, John and I went to the squadron command post to get answers. There we ran into the controller on duty who relayed commands. "Sorry, but the SAC order was placed on my desk just as they were bringing me my dinner, and I set the tray down on top of the message without reading it."

Nice!

CHAPTER 20

Cuban Missile Crisis

It was October 1962 when the US confirmed that there were Soviet missiles in Cuba. Marge was just being released from the base hospital, where she had undergone a major surgery on her left lung. I had been granted some time off to help her rehabilitate at home. The crisis changed that, and I was called back to the squadron after a few days as the crisis escalated. One mitigating factor was the fact that we lived on a street with families of crew members, and I thought I could count on Marge getting help from other wives.

When I went back to duty, I was more or less confined to the flight line. We got a SAC intelligence briefing every morning. The Airborne Alert was intensified and the bomb squadron called over to our squadron looking for spare pilots to fly as third pilot on the twenty-plus-hour mission in order to provide sleep time for overtaxed crew members. SAC's goal was to fill the skies around the periphery of the Soviet Union with nuclear-loaded bombers with a creditable reputation. I declined. The idea of spending twenty hours in a plane that I had never been in and about to go to war did not really appeal. I needed to save myself for what I was trained for.

Did it help? From what I could see and hear, I believe that this unprecedented threat was a game changer and not really, fully appreciated in the historical accounts of the situation.

To us and our families, this was a war about to begin. Ellsworth, I learned at the time, was rated as high on a Soviet target list. Probably sixth, due to the presence of not only a B-52 base but a nuclear weapons and missile storage facility. It was within range of the Cuban base missiles. Families started to evacuate the base. A lot of the wives took their kids and went to their family homes if they were from the West. Others took mattresses, bedding, and some camping things and went to the Black Hills.

A good friend of ours said she was staying to help Marge.

The negotiations between Kennedy and Khrushchev escalated to a fever like pitch it seemed. The ships had to turn around by a certain time, or all bets were off. We waited on pins and needles in the squadron building. We put on our sidearms, which we would carry on a war mission.

I was able to reach Marge on the phone. She could barely get to it to answer. Her friend had gotten in her car and left the base. She was alone with the kids, and she could barely take care of herself. I was beside myself. I had no choice.

The ships on the way to Cuba started to turn around. We were all sent to our planes and prepared to start engines. This was a trick by Khrushchev to put us off guard. That was the intelligence sent down from SAC. We sat in the planes and waited for the command to start engines. Time went by. Finally we got the word for all the crews to disembark the planes, except those that were scheduled for Alert anyway.

I went home and just in time. Marge needed help getting out of bed, forget the problem of taking care of the kids. I was upset about the choices I had. I was upset still about the earlier failure of the command post to give us the info we needed to stay alive. I was no longer career material.

Kennedy had, as part of the deal, agreed to ground all the B-47s in the SAC fleet. They were obsolete now and should have been grounded anyway. It was a good deal for the USA. However, it created a sudden glut of multi-engine jet pilots in SAC. The choice was to either transition to one of the aircraft being used in Vietnam or go home. I talked it over with Marge, and she wanted to go home, wherever that turned out to be. So did I.

I accepted an offer to resign my regular commission and return to my reserve commission. Then I would be processed out. I got a call from the Pentagon one morning thanking me for my service and telling me my papers would be there in two days.

We left Ellsworth with our heads up. Marge had shown she was the trooper I knew she was. When our neighbors returned, they could not apologize enough to Marge. I had contributed to the SAC mission as much as I could have been expected to.

I regret now that I did not make more of an effort to contact my old instructor, Mac, who had taught me the value of having a chip on my shoulder when I fly. I am now sure that the "chip" saved my life as well as my fellow crew members more than once.

ABOUT THE AUTHOR

Eugene Ross was born in 1934 in Oakland, California, with an identical twin, with his mother not surviving the childbirth and his twin brother passing away on a mutual hiking outing as adolescents. He was subsequently raised in several Southern California locations, including his high school days in Blythe, where he developed his love for aviation at the nearby desert airport. Following his late mother's footsteps, he attended UC Berkeley, studied urban land economics, participated in the then-required Air Force ROTC, was coxswain of the highly ranked crew team, and met the love of his life, partner, and wife, Marjorie. The experience of high school aviation and ROTC led him into pilot training and his journey in the USAF, leaving with the rank of captain. Following his departure from the Air Force in 1963, he moved to Martinez, California, with his wife, Marjorie, and two children, Mark and Marissa. He then pursued a career in real estate, forming a family firm with his wife and son, Mark. He also served his community with his distinguished twenty-year tenure as a trustee of the local community college district. Notably, the college district would name the boardroom after him upon retirement. Gene still serves the community to this day as a practicing realtor and property manager in Martinez.

www.ingramcontent.com/pod-product-compliance
Lightning Source LLC
Chambersburg PA
CBHW031350160726
47993CB00002B/899